I0020045

Integrating e-Portfolios into L2 Classrooms

NEW PERSPECTIVES ON LANGUAGE AND EDUCATION

Founding Editor: Viv Edwards, *University of Reading, UK*
Series Editors: Phan Le Ha, *University of Hawaii at Manoa, USA,* Joel Windle, *Monash University, Australia* and Kyle R. McIntosh, *University of Tampa*, USA.

Two decades of research and development in language and literacy education have yielded a broad, multidisciplinary focus. Yet education systems face constant economic and technological change, with attendant issues of identity and power, community and culture. What are the implications for language education of new 'semiotic economies' and communications technologies? Of complex blendings of cultural and linguistic diversity in communities and institutions? Of new cultural, regional and national identities and practices? The New Perspectives on Language and Education series will feature critical and interpretive, disciplinary and multidisciplinary perspectives on teaching and learning, language and literacy in new times. New proposals, particularly for edited volumes, are expected to acknowledge and include perspectives from the Global South. Contributions from scholars from the Global South will be particularly sought out and welcomed, as well as those from marginalised communities within the Global North.

All books in this series are externally peer-reviewed.

Full details of all the books in this series and of all our other publications can be found on http://www.multilingual-matters.com, or by writing to Multilingual Matters, St Nicholas House, 31-34 High Street, Bristol, BS1 2AW, UK.

NEW PERSPECTIVES ON LANGUAGE AND EDUCATION: 121

Integrating e-Portfolios into L2 Classrooms

Education for Future

Ricky Lam

MULTILINGUAL MATTERS
Bristol • Jackson

DOI https://doi.org/10.21832/LAM5805
Library of Congress Cataloging in Publication Data
A catalog record for this book is available from the Library of Congress.
Names: Lam, Ricky, author.
Title: Integrating e-Portfolios into L2 Classrooms: Education for Future/Ricky Lam.
Description: Bristol; Jackson: Multilingual Matters, 2024. | Series: New Perspectives
  on Language and Education: 121 | Includes bibliographical references and index.
  | Summary: "This book explains both the theory and practice of e-Portfolio
  pedagogy and assessment in second and foreign language classroom contexts. In
  addition to providing new insights for scholars of language pedagogy, the book
  equips language teachers with the practical knowledge and skills they need to use
  the e-Portfolio approach in their classrooms"– Provided by publisher.
Identifiers: LCCN 2024006354 (print) | LCCN 2024006355 (ebook) |
  ISBN 9781800415805 (hardback) | ISBN 9781800415799 (paperback) |
  ISBN 9781800415829 (epub) | ISBN 9781800415812 (pdf)
Subjects: LCSH: Language and languages–Computer-assisted instruction. |
  Electronic portfolios in education.
Classification: LCC P53.28 .L28 2024 (print) | LCC P53.28 (ebook) |
  DDC 418.0078/5–dc23/eng/20240317
LC record available at https://lccn.loc.gov/2024006354
LC ebook record available at https://lccn.loc.gov/2024006355

British Library Cataloguing in Publication Data
A catalogue entry for this book is available from the British Library.

ISBN-13: 978-1-80041-580-5 (hbk)
ISBN-13: 978-1-80041-579-9 (pbk)

Multilingual Matters
UK: St Nicholas House, 31-34 High Street, Bristol, BS1 2AW, UK.
USA: Ingram, Jackson, TN, USA.

Website: https://www.multilingual-matters.com
X: Multi_Ling_Mat
Facebook: https://www.facebook.com/multilingualmatters
Blog: https://www.channelviewpublications.wordpress.com

Copyright © 2024 Ricky Lam.

All rights reserved. No part of this work may be reproduced in any form or by any
means without permission in writing from the publisher.

The policy of Multilingual Matters/Channel View Publications is to use papers
that are natural, renewable and recyclable products, made from wood grown in
sustainable forests. In the manufacturing process of our books, and to further
support our policy, preference is given to printers that have FSC and PEFC Chain
of Custody certification. The FSC and/or PEFC logos will appear on those books
where full certification has been granted to the printer concerned.

Typeset by Deanta Global Publishing Services, Chennai, India.

Contents

Preface

Background

In this prelude, portfolio-related terminologies, such as paper-based portfolios, e-Portfolios (aka digital portfolios), portfolio assessment and formative and summative assessment are defined. A paper-based portfolio refers to a dossier in which students collect, select and self-assess different genres of artefacts in order to demonstrate their efforts, development and achievements over time. Similarly, an e-Portfolio is regarded as a digital container, where students create, compile, curate and reflect upon their multimodal artefacts to share with a target audience, namely teachers, parents, peers, netizens and/or admissions officers. Portfolio assessment usually involves teachers using either paper-based portfolios or e-Portfolios to assess students' performance for learning, grading and/or auditing purposes. It is apparent that e-Portfolios were a natural successor to paper-based portfolios at the turn of the century owing to the rapid growth of e-learning as a major curriculum reform agenda and the arrival of the World Wide Web. In certain educational contexts, both paper-based portfolios and e-Portfolios are being utilised concurrently for a number of reasons, including inadequate teacher training, obsolete curriculum design, limited resource allocation, public health issues (the COVID-19 pandemic) and natural disasters (Daniel, 2020).

Portfolios have been widely adopted in multiple disciplines, including art and design, architecture, nursing, teacher education and engineering over the past three decades. Their popularity is due to the fact that they serve as a handy method to support teaching, learning and assessment in a transparent and sustainable manner (Clarke & Boud, 2018). Portfolios help students review and reflect upon their learning, which is conducive to deep learning and the effective uptake of metacognitive learning strategies, such as goal setting, monitoring and adjusting (Bowman *et al.*, 2016). They also foster ownership, learning development, autonomy, reflection and collaboration at both course and programme level. In language education, paper-based portfolios and e-Portfolios are mainly applied in first (L1) and second language (L2) writing classrooms.

This is because the portfolio-based approach dovetails with the process writing approach, both of which came into prominence near the end of the 1980s (Lam, 2017). In fact, both approaches have much in common. For instance, they emphasise the learning process not product; nurture active not passive thinking; promote learner-centric not teacher-centric curriculum; and augment not restricting learning opportunities via text revision (Li, 2017).

As previously said, portfolios can be used for language teaching, learning and assessment. Concerning language teaching, portfolios facilitate process-orientated pedagogy and competency-based curricula, especially when major language competency skills are directly incorporated into portfolio tasks. As to language learning, portfolios nurture students' creativity, metacognition, critical thinking skills and digital literacy when they compile their paper-based portfolios or e-Portfolios within a community of practice. Regarding language assessment, albeit less reliable, portfolios fulfil formative assessment purposes much more effectively than summative assessment purposes, given that e-Portfolios are designed for enhancing learning through timely feedback and remediation rather than evaluating students' learning summatively (Lam, 2020). When implemented as a classroom-based assessment method, portfolio assessment performs multiple assessment functions, namely formative, summative, diagnostic and evaluative assessment. Formative assessment refers to iterative feedback processes that assist students to improve their language learning. The mode of feedback involves textual, audio, synchronous (e.g. live chats) or asynchronous (e.g. emails or forum messages). Summative assessment refers to the formal evaluation of students' learning near the end of a teaching unit or a school term. The mode of feedback entails letter grades, numerical scores or percentages. Diagnostic assessment refers to pre-assessment tasks, be they formative or summative, which inform how teachers plan or adjust their pedagogies based upon students' initial competency levels. Evaluative assessment is used to measure school performance as a whole and students' assessment information is presented as aggregate data to constitute parts of mandated external school reviews.

Following the global trend of curriculum reform, the Education Bureau (the Ministry of Education in Hong Kong) has started advocating assessment for/as learning practices, because the Hong Kong government is determined to promote an assessment culture to reduce the stakes of public exams at Grades 3, 6, 9 and 12 (Curriculum Development Council, 2017). In educational assessment, three chief purposes of assessment prevail, namely assessment of learning, assessment for learning and assessment as learning. Assessment of learning refers to the formal evaluation of students' learning, whereas assessment for learning is about effective classroom instruction highlighting the provision of timely feedback and interactive teaching practices to help close students' learning gaps against success criteria. Assessment as learning underscores the importance of self-assessment and self-reflection, which could facilitate learning-how-to-learn skills. It is typically regarded as a subset of assessment for learning. Since assessment of learning tends to be predominant, authentic assessment such as school-based assessment in the English language was introduced to support assessment for learning practices in 2007 (Davison & Leung, 2009). Since then, authentic assessment emphasising assessment for/as learning has been gradually experimented. One prominent form of authentic assessment is e-Portfolio use in Hong Kong English language classrooms as demonstrated in the author's recent research projects (see Chapters 6 and 7).

In sum, this prelude introduced what paper-based portfolios and e-Portfolios mean and their roles in language classrooms. It provided definitions of various portfolio-related jargon in context, which was likely to enhance readers' understanding. The preamble then explained why the Education Bureau in Hong Kong has promoted an assessment culture and e-Portfolio use at the classroom level.

1 Introduction

Introduction

Chapter 1, the opening chapter, sets the scene for the entire book. It recounts the origin of paper-based portfolios and then describes how they transitioned into the digital medium near the turn of the century. Afterwards, it introduces various types and mediums of e-Portfolios and their pros and cons. Chapter 1 then discusses the role of e-Portfolios in general education and second language (L2) writing classrooms. In conclusion, it reveals the aims, focus and structure of the book and explains how this monograph can fulfil the different needs of prospective readers.

From Paper-Based to Electronic Portfolios

Portfolios were originally used in other professions, such as visual arts, architecture, photography and medical education. In general education, they were used as a learning method, and assisted students to continuously organise, manage and review their learning for knowledge advancement. Portfolio use in language education was first adopted in university classrooms in the late 1980s. At that time, writing faculties observed that assessing first-year university students with timed essay tests created many issues (e.g. high failure and dropout rates); therefore, programme directors attempted to substitute one-off impromptu tests with writing portfolios as an exit requirement for first-year writing programmes (Belanoff & Dickson, 1991). Since then, writing portfolios or portfolios have been extensively implemented to achieve both formative and summative assessment purposes in higher education. For instance, portfolios are well known for serving as a running record to showcase students' milestones in teaching practicum, overseas immersion programmes, interdisciplinary projects, experiential learning ventures and related co-curricular activities (Barrett, 2007; Chaudhuri & Cabau, 2018).

In K-12 school settings, portfolios were used as a 'better' alternative to supplement the predominant product-based pedagogies, in which multi-drafting, peer response and self-assessment were rarely practiced.

When portfolios were initially applied at the classroom level, they were considered a learning-driven and process-orientated instructional approach. In the 1990s, in certain first language (L1) classroom settings, teachers innovated their writing instruction by introducing the portfolio approach to help students overcome writing anxiety (i.e. writer's block) and difficulties (i.e. mastery of specific genre structures; Hamp-Lyons & Condon, 2000). Because of their educational merits, a number of districts in the United States started using writing portfolios as a standardised assessment method. However, after a two-year pilot in two states, graded portfolio assessment was proven untrustworthy statistically due to low inter-rater reliability, not to mention the complexity of portfolio scoring and the cost incurred by such a labour-intensive scoring method (Koretz, 1998; Scott, 2005). Henceforth, scholars have claimed that portfolios are best suited to supporting formative assessment practices, namely student self-assessment and self-reflection in writing classrooms (Mak & Wong, 2018).

During the heyday of writing portfolios, many educators jumped on the bandwagon. At the turn of the century, with stable wifi connection and the advent of user-friendly digital gadgets, some schools migrated from their paper-based portfolio programmes to digital ones. However, scholars realised that some simply changed the medium without altering the purpose, outcomes and evaluation methods of their new e-Portfolio programmes. This phenomenon implied that teachers' limited pedagogical knowledge remained a cause for concern when paper-based portfolio programmes were innovated (Yancey, 2001). In classroom settings, teachers encouraged students to convert their paper-based portfolios to electronic ones by utilising institutional intranet systems, open source platforms, word processing or presentation software. Such classroom-level transition usually took place gradually and contextually, so that students could improve their learning more efficiently with e-Portfolios (Springfield, 2001). That said, research showed that teachers and students encountered numerous barriers when their portfolio programmes were digitalised, including low computer literacy, inadequate infrastructure and lack of coherent planning in this daunting undertaking (cf. Siu, 2013; Woodward & Nanlohy, 2004). The next section describes different types and formats of e-Portfolios.

Types and Mediums of e-Portfolios

In the professional literature, there are three types of e-Portfolios: working, showcasing and assessment e-Portfolios (Stefani et al., 2007). Working e-Portfolios focus on how students compile and develop their e-Portfolios in a sustained and longitudinal manner. This type of e-Portfolio is learning orientated, personalised and autobiographical. Showcasing e-Portfolios highlight students' accomplishments through demonstrating their best artefacts and representative works to target audiences, e.g. future employers, university admissions officers and potential clients. This type of e-Portfolio is typically pragmatic, outcome based and product orientated. Assessment e-Portfolios, as their name suggests, entail a summative evaluation of students' learning for accountability purposes. This e-Portfolio type tends to be restrictive in content because it needs to align with official assessment criteria and appraisal frameworks. It is also high-stakes because the assessment results will affect students' future study and professional careers. It appears that working e-Portfolios are suitable for individualised learning, whereas showcasing and assessment e-Portfolios are, by default, course based and programme based as they are formally evaluated by teachers and audited by school senior management.

The mediums of e-Portfolios include (1) print version uploaded on the intranet (e.g. e-Class); (2) open source platforms (e.g. Moodle); (3) web-based portfolio software (e.g. WordPress and Seesaw); and (4) social media (e.g. Facebook and Instagram; Belgrad, 2013). The simplest version is (1). In the case of students in junior forms who do not possess a high level of digital literacy, teachers can assist them to key their hand-written drafts into a word processing programme or presentation software for portfolio compilation. For (2) and (3), students are required to manage the interfaces of those open source platforms. Albeit user-friendly, teachers may still need to coach students on how to use those basic functions before they can manipulate the e-Portfolio platform or web-based portfolio software independently. For (4), although school-level students are probably quite familiar with the use of social media platforms, they may only get to know more up-to-date sites like TikTok and Instagram than Facebook, since the latter is commonly used among adults. The next section details the pros and cons of e-Portfolio use.

Pros and Cons

The pros of e-Portfolios are (a) accessibility, (b) visibility and (c) storage. Accessibility refers to the extent to which students, teachers and parents can access students' e-Portfolios for reviewing, commenting and communicating. Unquestionably, students can compile their e-Portfolios on- and off-campus as long as they can access their electronic gadgets and a wifi connection. Teachers and parents can monitor and check on students' learning progress anytime and anywhere (Lam, 2023). Visibility is about how intended audiences can view students' e-Portfolios online. Since e-Portfolios are mostly web based, they enable students to express their ideas openly, make their thinking visible and narrate their learning journeys in hypertextual formats. Students can view each other's language profiles online to celebrate their achievements and to conduct formative assessments for learning improvement (e.g. peer response;

Renwick, 2017), whereas parents and teachers can appreciate and encourage students' e-Portfolio compilation. Storage alludes to the digital space that students can utilise to host their multimedia artefacts. Unlike paper-based portfolios, students can upload numerous files to their e-Portfolio accounts for compilation, provided that they do not exceed the default memory capacity of the system. In this regard, e-Portfolios have the edge over paper-based portfolios, especially when students can retain their e-Portfolio contents across grade levels (Wuetherick & Dickinson, 2015).

The disadvantages of e-Portfolios include (1) computer literacy, (2) digital divide and (3) privacy. Since mastering e-Portfolio applications demands knowledge and skills, teachers and students need to attain a specific level of computer literacy in order to use e-Portfolios effectively. The acquisition of computer literacy requires time and effort. Without adequate computer literacy, any e-Portfolio integration is doomed to failure (Cummins & Davesne, 2009). Another concern is the digital divide. Although e-learning has been popular in language education, not every student has the privilege to own a tablet or an internet-connected mobile phone for flipped learning. E-Portfolio implementations may further widen the gap of this divide, creating unnecessary inequality in educational opportunities and discrimination against those who are socioeconomically disadvantaged (Rafalow & Puckett, 2022). Because school students are minors, the privacy of e-Portfolios is a thorny issue to handle. When students are required to compose reflective pieces for e-Portfolios, they may unconsciously disclose some sensitive personal data, such as health issues, academic aptitudes, family background or personal struggles. If this confidential information is leaked, students are likely to be traumatised by public humiliation and become easy targets of online harassment (Wilson et al., 2018). The following section discusses the role of e-Portfolios in general education and L2 writing classrooms.

Role of e-Portfolios in Education

In universities, the implementation of interdisciplinary pedagogy, lifelong learning and authentic assessment has been commonplace in various educational jurisdictions. The incorporation of e-Portfolios into general education/subject curricula facilitates broad-based learning, critical thinking, as well as active knowledge building when students compile their digital artefacts to support integrative learning throughout their undergraduate studies and beyond (Light et al., 2012). In other words, not only do e-Portfolios serve as an instructional method to explore students' learning potentials to the full, but they are also utilised as a virtual communal learning space that connects academic and co-curricular activities, formal and informal learning, pedagogies and assessment in a holistic and unobtrusive manner. The role of e-Portfolios in general education could be described as central and essential rather than peripheral and haphazard in terms of helping students to thrive and accomplish in their study careers. Nonetheless, given the flexibility and relatively easy start-up of e-Portfolios, they have the potential to be adopted in all sorts of educational environments where academic levels, purposes, settings and curricula may vary diversely and where integrative education, reflective learning and authentic assessment are not necessarily prioritised (Eynon & Gambino, 2017).

In L2 writing classrooms, e-Portfolios serve as a user-friendly companion to promote various aspects of students' writing development. Affectively, e-Portfolios enable students to become confident, independent and self-efficacious throughout the portfolio construction process (Aygün & Aydin, 2016). Linguistically, e-Portfolios help students to improve their accuracy, fluency, vocabulary learning and peer feedback skills (Barrot, 2021). Metacognitively, e-Portfolios support the acquisition of self-assessment and self-regulated learning skills, especially in those portfolio programmes featuring self-reflection (Segaran & Hasim, 2021). In addition, e-Portfolios in L2 writing classrooms act as a catalyst to promote active student agency, since students need to take the lead role when creating, curating, reviewing, plus publishing digital artefacts and disseminating them to new audiences. Such novel e-Portfolio experience and innovative exploration facilitate a paradigm shift in remote pedagogies (e.g. shared expertise and the co-construction of knowledge with and by students) and online learning (i.e. new reading and composing processes – flipped learning and synchronous collaborative writing; Fathi & Rahimi, 2022). This pedagogical paradigm shift redefines a new relationship between process and product in L2 writing classrooms. This is because the role of e-Portfolios empowers students to focus on the composing and revision (acts of reflection) processes more than the final written products (Yancey, 1996). The penultimate section details the aims, focus and structure of this book.

Aims, Focus and Structure of the Book

The aims of this book are fourfold. It intends (1) to advance scholars' research insights and epistemological foundation when they investigate the affective, linguistic and metacognitive aspects of e-Portfolios in L2 classrooms; (2) to equip language teachers with the knowledge and skills when they attempt e-Portfolios for instruction in their work contexts; (3) to broaden major stakeholders' knowledge base about e-Portfolio assessment literacy, including staff members from the Ministry of Education, language testers, curriculum planners and school middle management personnel because they make significant decisions on curriculum design and assessment practices; and (4) to increase postgraduate students' academic exposure, since they may develop a better understanding of how classroom-based assessment research is conducted in the author's case studies. The focus of the book emphasises a healthy balance between the theory, research and practice of e-Portfolio integration, which can inform effective L2 instruction and assessment as well as enhance major stakeholders' language assessment literacy.

The book has a preamble and nine chapters. The prelude familiarises readers with definitions and basic concepts. Chapter 1 described the different types and mediums of e-Portfolios, their pros and cons and the role of e-Portfolios in education. Chapter 2 identifies the emerging themes by reviewing e-Portfolio-based research over the past two decades. Chapter 3 unpacks the theoretical rationale for e-Portfolios by discussing the theories of socio-constructivism, assessment for learning and metacognition. Chapter 4 discusses how teachers integrate various e-Portfolio approaches into mainstream English language curricula. Chapter 5 demonstrates how e-Portfolios can achieve formative and summative assessment purposes in the L2 classroom contexts, and how teachers can adopt e-Portfolios to promote assessment for/as learning practices. Chapter 6 reports on a case study about adolescent students' perceptions of and engagement in e-Portfolio compilation in two Hong Kong secondary schools. Chapter 7 presents another case study concerning how two Hong Kong English language teachers tried out e-Portfolios in remote teaching during the pandemic and beyond. Chapter 8 reviews the functionalities and practicalities of common digital tools that could be used as customised e-Portfolio platforms. Lastly, Chapter 9 discusses the future directions of e-Portfolio application and research and provides a supplementary resource section for readers if they plan to start up or sustain e-Portfolio integration in L2 contexts.

Summary

Chapter 1 introduced the origins of paper-based and electronic portfolios. It then described various types and mediums of e-Portfolios, followed by a discussion of their pros and cons. The chapter subsequently explained the role of e-Portfolios in general education and L2 writing classroom contexts. To conclude, Chapter 1 introduced the aims, focus and structure of the book to prospective readers.

2 Review of Portfolio-Based Scholarship

Introduction

Chapter 2 is a literature review of the book. It evaluates state-of-the-art portfolio-based studies and identifies the overall e-Portfolio trend in language education. It first presents various types and aspects of e-Portfolio-related scholarship in general education and in second language (L2) writing classrooms. It then discusses three prominent themes of e-Portfolio research: process, product and tool. Furthermore, Chapter 2 reviews e-Portfolio-related studies in terms of teaching, learning and assessment at various educational levels and in multiple geographical regions. To conclude, it identifies and addresses up-and-coming e-Portfolio research agendas.

Types and Aspects of e-Portfolio-Related Studies

Like most educational research, e-Portfolio-related studies are broadly categorised into three types: professional, empirical and theoretical (e.g. literature reviews) scholarship. Professional e-Portfolio scholarship refers to practically orientated instructional guides or academic textbooks that provide step-by-step procedures and authentic classroom examples for educator readers who plan to adopt e-Portfolios (cf. Renwick, 2017). Empirical e-Portfolio research refers to rigorous studies employing qualitative, quantitative or mixed methods to investigate the impacts of e-Portfolio interventions on students' learning (cf. Pourdana & Tavassoli, 2022). Theoretical scholarship refers to systematic or scoping review studies that survey the e-Portfolio landscape in order to identify emerging topics for future scholarly investigations (cf. Lam, 2023). The studies reviewed in this chapter are derived from empirical and theoretical scholarship conducted over the past 20 years.

A decade ago, two early theoretical studies reviewed the transition from paper-based to electronic portfolios. Both evaluated the benefits and shortcomings of e-Portfolios and revealed the implementation barriers when they were applied in classroom settings. The first study was a multidisciplinary literature review looking into various disciplines, namely teacher education, nursing, medicine and others (Butler, 2006). The review was descriptive, informational and instructional despite the fact that the author did not explicitly discuss the inclusion criteria for selecting those papers under review. The second study reviewed the scholarship of paper-based and electronic portfolios based upon three action research projects conducted in the United States (Belgrad, 2013). The author emphasised the importance of promoting student reflection on multimedia artefacts and a culture of evidence in both portfolio mediums. However, the author did not describe the nuts and bolts of actual e-Portfolio implementation in L2 classroom contexts nor did she mention any pedagogical implications for classroom teachers.

Bryant and Chittum (2013) published a systematic review study that surveyed e-Portfolio scholarship published between 1996 and 2012. Their findings categorised four types of e-Portfolio-related studies: (1) descriptive (42%); (2) empirical, affective (34%); (3) empirical, outcomes (15%); and (4) technological (9%; Bryant & Chittum, 2013: 190). Type (1) studies refer to research that reported on secondary data relating to how e-Portfolios were applied and managed. Type (2) studies refer to empirical studies that investigated students' perceptions of e-Portfolio learning. Type (3) studies also refer to empirical studies that examined the impacts of e-Portfolios on students' learning via qualitative or quantitative methods. Type (4) studies resemble a technological brief of the latest e-Portfolio software that describes its usage and functions. Types (1) and (4) studies are synonymous with e-Portfolio professional scholarship without presenting original data, whereas Types (2) and (3) studies equate to e-Portfolio empirical and theoretical scholarship that includes proper methodologies and research questions generating original data. Thus far, Bryant and Chittum's review study has been the most comprehensive, providing e-Portfolio advocates with evidence-based research insights and directions. For instance, there is an urgent need for more empirical studies, particularly 'outcomes' studies for researchers, and technological studies for teachers.

More recently, Lam (2023) conducted a thematic review by evaluating (1) work done extensively, (2) work done inadequately and (3) work to be done in e-Portfolio pedagogy and assessment. Lam's review study can be classified as one example of theoretical scholarship as described at the beginning of this section. Lam (2023) reviewed 70 research outputs and coded 13 categories according to the aforementioned three broad themes. In Theme (1), much has been done to examine (a) learning gains, (b) improvement in language sub-skills, (c) self-regulated learning, (d) perceptions of e-Portfolios and (e) effectiveness of e-Portfolio applications. In Theme (2), little has been done to investigate (f) compilation experience, (g) longitudinal studies, (h) challenges to manoeuvre e-Portfolio interfaces, (i) resources best supporting self-reflection and (j) e-Portfolio assessment literacy. Theme (3) reveals what needs to be explored, including (k) use of social media as e-Portfolios, (l) adoption of e-Portfolios to align formative and summative assessment and (m) e-Portfolios as high-stakes testing. Although Lam's study does not review those outputs according to e-Portfolio types such as professional, empirical and theoretical scholarship, it definitely identifies updated research agendas that enable other researchers to examine e-Portfolio-related issues from new perspectives.

After surveying three common types of e-Portfolio studies, the chapter now reviews various aspects of e-Portfolio studies. Of these, teachers and researchers tend to investigate the following aspects: autonomy, motivation, writing performance, metacognition, ownership and collaboration. When scholars researched into the aforementioned aspects, they usually implemented an e-Portfolio intervention programme and then measured its impacts on students' learning after 10–16 weeks, depending on the scope of the programme and learners' educational levels. As to autonomy, students were more likely to become independent in L2 learning, especially when actively engaged in e-Portfolio compilation though not without challenges (Hung & Huang, 2010). Regarding motivation, some studies found that a majority of students became more motivated towards writing while they were constructing their e-Portfolios with teachers' input (Cho, 2018). Writing performance is one of the most controversial areas of investigation, wherein students generally did not have noticeable writing improvement even after exposure to an e-Portfolio programme (cf. Driessen *et al.*, 2007). As to metacognition, evidence has shown that the reflective components in paper-based and electronic portfolios could assist students to become self-reflective and self-regulated in language learning (Farahian *et al.*, 2021). Ownership is another thorny issue because it remains unclear whether students' ownership could be enhanced during or after the e-Portfolio compilation process, especially in those two- to six-week short-term projects (Yancey, 2019). Considering collaboration, L2 writing research indicated that e-Portfolios facilitated the mastery of peer assessment and collaborative writing skills, if only partially (Allal, 2021). The next section reviews three salient themes of e-Portfolio research.

Themes of e-Portfolio Research

As stated by Alvarez and Moxley (2004), e-Portfolios entail process, product and tool, inferring that they represent ongoing instructional processes, final learning outcomes and applications of digital software tools, respectively. Process refers to studies that reported on students' e-Portfolio compilation experience and procedures, and teachers' attempts at trying out classroom-based e-Portfolio programmes. Product refers to research that measured the impacts of e-Portfolio interventions on students' language learning and mastery of self-reflective skills.

Tool refers to studies that described the usefulness of any e-Portfolio applications as a mode of pedagogical plus assessment method by teachers, researchers and language specialists. Each of the following sub-sections review e-Portfolio scholarship in relation to these three components, namely process, product and tool.

Process

E-Portfolio-related studies with the process attribute include (1) transition from one portfolio medium to another, (2) students' emotional experience when compiling e-Portfolios, (3) e-Portfolio use from one educational level to another, (4) longitudinal study and (5) e-Portfolio development procedures. Theme (1) reveals how students responded to the transition from paper-based to electronic portfolios in a course or a programme. The findings showed that a majority of student informants preferred e-Portfolios to paper-based counterparts, since the former enhanced self-reflective skills, audience awareness and new digital identities (e.g. Barrot, 2021; Clark, 2010; Woodward & Nanlohy, 2004). Except for Bowman *et al.*'s (2016) study, it demonstrated that university freshmen considered paper-based and digital portfolios equally useful in helping them to integrate learning across different courses. Theme (2) reports on students' emotional experience when they compiled their e-Portfolios. Students' emotions and attitudes towards e-Portfolios were mixed. The positive results revealed that the students could make substantial improvements in their language skills (i.e. reading, writing, grammar and vocabulary), research skills and critical thinking skills, whereas the negative results highlighted that the students found portfolio keeping boring and time-consuming (Aydin, 2014; Barrot, 2016). In addition, some students had anxiety after participating in the e-Portfolio programme and resisted using technology in L2 learning (Hung, 2012).

Theme (3) is about studies that tracked students' use of e-Portfolios from one educational level to another. The findings of two studies confirmed that students' ongoing writing development could be accurately captured and transferred from high school to university settings. Faculty members were able to develop a better understanding of students' learning trajectories, although the authors emphasised more teacher–faculty communications were needed to facilitate further cross-sectoral e-Portfolio studies (Acker & Halasek, 2008; Fahey *et al.*, 2007). Theme (4) refers to longitudinal studies, which usually last for more than one year. Clancy and Gardner (2017) carried out a three-year longitudinal study on participants with special educational needs. The results showed that the quality of students' e-Portfolios in Year 3 (69%) was much better than in Year 2 (38%). The authors suggested that teachers receive more training in assessing non-academic skills (e.g. life skills) and digitalising work for students using multimedia formats. Theme (5) shows how students perceived and experienced their e-Portfolio development processes. In a pilot study, Wuetherick and Dickinson (2015) administered an online questionnaire to 218 continuing education students. The respondents provided numerous constructive recommendations alongside concerns before the actual e-Portfolio programme was launched. Likewise, Hung and Huang (2010) reported on how three university-level students utilised a web blog-based e-Portfolio platform as coursework in one 18-week semester. The informants could enhance their metacognitive awareness in learning but were unable to practice self and peer assessments because of their limited English proficiency.

Product

E-Portfolio-related studies measuring the products of learning entail (i) the effects of e-Portfolios on students' language learning, (ii) the impacts of e-Portfolios on students' acquisition of self-reflective skills and (iii) how and whether an e-Portfolio intervention can promote reflection and/or peer assessment skills. Studies in Theme (i) showed that student participants had improved their language learning after adopting e-Portfolios. In a quasi-experimental study, Händel et al. (2020) proved that university-level students in an experimental group using e-Portfolios obtained higher exam scores than those in a control group without using e-Portfolios because the former group regularly adopted cognitive learning strategies during the nine-week course. In their quantitative study using a questionnaire instrument, Cheng and Chau (2013) corroborated that 26 university-level informants, who frequently mobilised metacognitive and collaborative strategies, obtained higher e-Portfolio scores. Similarly, Al-Qallaf and Al-Mutairi (2016) found that 23 5th graders had marked improvement in sentence length, spelling and grammatical accuracy after their exposure to a web blog e-Portfolio programme.

Theme (ii) refers to the impacts of e-Portfolios on students' mastery of self-reflective skills. In their quasi-experimental study, Sharifi et al. (2017) identified that e-Portfolios had a substantial impact on 66 informants' vocabulary learning. At the end of the study, the informants had marked improvement in their metacognitive strategy awareness and self-assessment skills. In two other mixed-methods studies, the authors noticed that the implementation of e-Portfolios could motivate students towards language learning and facilitate the mastery of self-reflective skills. Cheng and Chau (2009) showed how 15 undergraduates adopted video-based self-reflection to improve their English proficiency on an e-Portfolio platform. De Bruin et al. (2012) demonstrated that 156 11th graders were motivated to engage in self-reflective practices for their portfolios. One limitation of these two studies is that e-Portfolios mainly motivated students to be self-reflective but were unable to help them engage in deep reflection.

Theme (iii) refers to whether an e-Portfolio programme can support student reflection and peer feedback skills. Nicol *et al.* (2019) investigated whether introducing peer review could promote reflection. The authors verified that reflection assisted 19 master's degree students to self and peer evaluate their portfolio works at the analytical level. The quality of the informants' portfolios was much better than those in the previous year. The authors concluded that e-Portfolios emphasising reflection could help promote not only self-reflective skills, but also peer review skills. In another study, Bader *et al.* (2019) investigated the role of formative feedback in writing portfolios among 40 pre-service teachers. The findings showed that the informants had positive attitudes towards teacher and peer feedback and appreciated the opportunities to revise works in progress with either feedback source. Nevertheless, they preferred teacher feedback to peer feedback because they considered the latter less 'constructive' for revision. The authors also implied that the informants remained optimistic about peer discussions for their group projects and enjoyed participating in peer review activities.

Tool

Studies that reviewed e-Portfolio tools examined the following aspects: (a) implementation logistics and barriers, (b) pros and cons and (c) sustainability. Siu (2013) reported on how she implemented a large-scale e-Portfolio programme for 1500 undergraduates in a comprehensive university. The study described the trial procedures in three executive semesters. Most content-related and technical issues were resolved after the programme team migrated from one learning management system to another, namely from Blackboard to Google Sites. Siu's (2013) study primarily focused on the logistics and barriers she encountered when she created, innovated and developed the new e-Portfolio software. Likewise, Karlin *et al.* (2016) investigated how three K-12 teachers tried out three e-Portfolio platforms in their classrooms, namely Wix (a Web 2.0 tool), Schoology (a learning management system) and Google Sites (a free web-based application). The authors compared and contrasted the pros and cons of these three e-Portfolio applications and suggested a thorough review between the advantages of free and subscription-based e-Portfolio programmes. To promote sustainability in e-Portfolio development, Shepherd and Skrabut (2011) claimed that the use of a personal learning environment (PLE) as an e-Portfolio site was a better alternative to an open-source e-Portfolio software application. They argued that PLE-based e-Portfolios had three benefits, including the promotion of learner autonomy, self-reflective practices and integrative learning across disciplines and educational levels. However, the authors cautioned that teachers needed to seriously consider software selection, training, rubric construction and collaboration when adopting PLE-based e-Portfolios owing to their complexity and versatility. The subsequent section discusses e-Portfolio scholarship in L2 education with reference to teaching, learning and assessment.

E-Portfolio Scholarship in L2 Education

Teaching

Situated in L2 pedagogical contexts, e-Portfolios are recognised as an alternative instructional method to supplement face-to-face language teaching owing to their multimedia and interactive nature. They can be flexibly adopted in flipped classroom teaching, emergency remote teaching and mixed-mode instruction (i.e. blended learning methods; Lam, 2022). Although e-Portfolio pedagogy has become increasingly popular, scholars have warned that teachers need to transform their beliefs, practices and understanding of English language teaching, especially when they take on new roles and identities in this emerging instructional method (Yancey, 2004). Additionally, teachers and students are expected to attain a certain level of digital literacy before they are ready to participate in an e-Portfolio programme effectively (Al Kahtani, 1999). Not only does e-Portfolio instruction expect renewed pedagogical knowledge, but it also requires technological know-how to manoeuvre the fundamental operations of an e-Portfolio application (Sasai, 2017).

Teachers often use e-Portfolios to teach literacy skills (i.e. reading and writing) and vocabulary skills to school students, particularly L2 writing skills that have been extensively researched (Lam, 2023). A majority of these studies investigated how and whether e-Portfolios, as a new teaching method, could help promote students' writing development (peer feedback skills; Nicol *et al.*, 2019) and improve their written products (language accuracy; Barrot, 2021). They also looked into curriculum design, content coverage, portfolio processes, transition of portfolio medium and modes of delivery, e.g. synchronous and asynchronous before actual implementation (Aygün & Aydin, 2016). To further classify these studies, there are two broad categories when e-Portfolios are adopted as an instructional method: (1) large-scale national e-Portfolio projects and (2) context-specific classroom-based action research projects.

The first category includes two studies, namely a two-year action research project titled 'REFLECT Initiative'. It involved more than 20 districts and up to 6000 secondary-level students across the United States, investigating the impacts of e-Portfolios on student learning, motivation and engagement (Barrett, 2007). Another large-scale e-Portfolio project titled 'ePEARL' involved 16 elementary-level teachers and their Grades 4–6 students across three cities in Canada (Meyer *et al.*, 2011). These two classical studies identified a plethora of inhibiting factors when e-Portfolios were used for L1 and L2 teaching. The researchers observed that when the teacher participants lacked e-learning training, initiatives to change, the provision of infrastructure (e.g. stable wifi connection) and opportunities to master technological pedagogical skills, they would find e-Portfolio pedagogy less effective or even cumbersome to implement. Becker (2015) reported that a cross-national e-Portfolio project named 'European Language Portfolio' was not widely utilised by English language teachers in Europe as one of the legitimate instructional methods for two reasons: overreliance on textbooks and rigid lesson organisations that did not support the learner-centred portfolio curriculum.

The second category exemplifies two action research projects. Belgrad (2013) reported on three action research studies in US K-12 classrooms. The teachers-as-researchers raised concerns about the low level of student agency in the e-Portfolio processes. Belgrad (2013) suggested that teachers who attempted e-Portfolios consider encouraging students to convert multimedia artefacts into validated learning evidence via active self-assessment and self-reflection. She also proposed that teachers needed to promote a culture of evidence in order to substantiate effective learning in e-Portfolio pedagogy. Lam *et al.* (2023) described an action research project carried out by two English language teachers. Because of the COVID-19 pandemic, the two teacher informants implemented e-Portfolio pedagogy innovatively to survive four rounds of class suspension. In the study, the two teachers utilised the affordances of e-Portfolios (i.e. asynchronous communications and rapid feedback provision) to facilitate remote teaching for almost a year. This action research project is further elaborated on in Chapter 7.

Learning

When scholars investigate e-Portfolios and L2 learning, they focus on three aspects: (i) how e-Portfolios, as a facility, help students improve their writing skills, especially through weblogs; (ii) how e-Portfolios, as a learning strategy, enhance students' self-regulated learning abilities; and (iii) students' perceptions of e-Portfolio compilation and management experience in L2 learning. In (i), e-Portfolios are considered a learning facility to help students improve their writing through text revision over time. Weblogs are commonly adopted as a 'blog portfolio' in some studies. This digital tool facilitates process writing, collaborative writing and problem-solving skills. Daskalogiannaki (2012) investigated whether blogging could motivate English as a foreign language (EFL) writing and enhance learning engagement among 12 adolescent students. The results showed that the informants had a slight improvement in process writing (better peer editing skills), motivation for writing blogs (increased participation) and writing development (ability to compose longer and more complex texts). Similarly, Nicolaidou (2013) looked into whether the use of a weblog-based e-Portfolio platform (i.e. WordPress) could improve writing performance and peer feedback with 20 primary-level students. The findings indicated that the more-able students benefited more than their less-able counterparts in terms of writing improvement and mastery of peer feedback skills. In a blogging project, O'Byrne and Murrell (2014) reported that 51 11th graders could utilise blogs to enhance their multimodal literacies and considered blogs as a media-rich platform to create new knowledge. The findings also showed that learning through blogs enhanced peer interactions and increased student engagement in learning.

In (ii), Nicolaidou (2010) tried out weblogs as an e-Portfolio learning strategy to promote self-regulated learning in writing with three groups of 4th graders. The findings demonstrated that the e-Portfolio group outperformed the other two groups using paper-based portfolios. The high-performing students were able to set more goals and engaged in self-reflection more effectively. As to writing improvement, the informants could improve their essays across drafts, namely from the sixth to the eighth drafts. In Cheng and Chau's (2009) study, 15 post-secondary-level students were motivated to reflect on their learning by creating digital videos in e-Portfolios. Although the findings were encouraging, the students could not engage in a deeper level of reflection owing to inadequate self-regulated learning skills. Chang *et al.* (2018) explored how high school students using e-Portfolios to learn goal setting could influence their self-regulated learning. The experimental study proved that using e-Portfolios to practice goal setting impacted students' self-regulated learning skills, and the results also led to slightly better learning motivation, self-judgement and self-efficacy.

As to (iii), Baeten *et al.* (2008) examined how 138 university students perceived their learning preferences in a portfolio-based environment. Adopting the pre-test and post-test design with two scales, the authors found that students' surface approaches to learning increased significantly due to workload, motivation and use of learning strategies. The students did not experience the advantages of portfolio assessment nor did they prefer a deep approach to learning. McLaren (2012) utilised 'e-scape', an e-Portfolio platform to promote assessment for learning practices, such as focused scaffolding, sharing of success criteria and guided questions as feedback. The findings revealed that the students ($n = 305$) enjoyed peer learning and self-assessment in the e-Portfolio approach, and the teachers ($n = 5$) liked giving e-feedback to students to enhance their language learning. McLeod and Vasinda (2009) investigated various stakeholders' experience of and satisfaction with the e-Portfolio process in one elementary school. They identified that 64% of the students enjoyed the e-Portfolio learning process because they had fun, choice and autonomy to curate digital artefacts. Teachers felt that their students took ownership of their learning. Parents were equally satisfied with their children's reflective learning via audio self-reflection.

Assessment

Teachers have long used paper-based portfolios for the purpose of assessment. They have used portfolios as a substitute for placement assessments, exit language tests and large-scale public exams (Yancey & Weiser, 1997). In language assessment research, scholars have generally regarded e-Portfolios as a form of authentic assessment or alternative assessment, which is different from conventional in-person, paper-and-pen assessments (Cummins & Davesne, 2009). Used as an authentic assessment, e-Portfolios can evaluate creativity, metacognition, communication skills, cultural competence and problem-solving skills other than language proficiency only. While some studies indicate that paper-based or electronic portfolios are a better alternative to traditional one-off composition tests, others caution that there remains inadequate empirical evidence to substantiate this claim then and now (Yancey, 2019). In fact, scholars are aware that the use of e-Portfolios as a regular authentic assessment in L2 classrooms or standardised tests need to be evidently validated by sound language assessment principles (Abrar-ul-Hassan et al., 2021).

E-Portfolios can be used for formative and summative assessment. However, they fit in well more with the former than the latter because they entail numerous benefits to support students' L2 learning when applied pedagogically, such as the provision of instant and multimodal feedback to improve learning, opportunities to revise and resubmit works until satisfactory and conditions encouraging self-reflection for deep learning. Arguing against the use of a scoring guide to assess e-Portfolios, Yancey (2015) advocated conversations in scoring on top of the rubrics in order to give students feedback with a future focus, namely what they can accomplish in the next assignment tasks. Similarly, Barrett (2007) proposed that teachers needed to promote a culture of evidence by providing students with a supportive environment to self-reflect on their digital artefacts with sound justifications. The act of evidence-based reflective practices was likely to promote deep learning and critical thinking skills. A few studies also added that these formative assessment aspects of e-Portfolios could be best integrated with portfolio pedagogy to enhance students' language learning (Lam, 2019, 2021b).

In reality, e-Portfolios are summatively graded in school. Studies investigating the issues of e-Portfolio assessment identified that e-Portfolios defied scoring and it was taxing for teachers to grade e-Portfolios impartially, given their scope (multi-genres) and complexity (Stefani et al., 2007). Other studies showed that the cost and administrative procedures involved in scoring paper-based or electronic portfolios was exorbitant (McDonald, 2012). The implementation of large-scale portfolio assessment in the 1990s proved to achieve low scoring reliability, especially for inter-rater reliability (Scott, 2005). Because of this, researchers proposed that e-Portfolios were more contextually viable to be adopted as classroom-based formative assessment, in which multiple feedback sources could serve as a catalyst to support effective language instruction, namely process-orientated approaches to teaching and assessing L2 writing (Gu, 2021). Some scholars have claimed that if e-Portfolios were used to fulfil external standards for competency, their learning and reflective potentials would be largely diminished (Butler, 2006). They also pointed out that there was always a trade-off when teachers used e-Portfolios to achieve assessment for learning and assessment of learning simultaneously, not to mention that the latter tended to overshadow the former because of a deep-seated exam-driven culture (Lee, 2021a). Utilising e-Portfolios as an assessment method is further discussed in Chapter 5. In regard to the aforementioned review, the last section discusses emerging e-Portfolio-related research agendas.

Emerging Research Agendas to be Addressed

The first emerging research agenda is related to the types and aspects of e-Portfolio research. The first section of this chapter indicates that there is adequate empirical research (i.e. empirical affective) but insufficient theoretical research in overall e-Portfolio scholarship, such as literature review studies. Thus far, there are four major e-Portfolio review studies, including Butler (2006), Belgrad (2013), Bryant and Chittum (2013) and Lam (2023). Of them, Bryant and Chittum (2013) is the only systematic one that comprehensively examined various types of e-Portfolio research, but it was published a decade ago. To this end, one forthcoming research agenda is to conduct more systematic review studies that can track ongoing e-Portfolio trends and developments and the impacts on teacher professional development. This body of e-Portfolio research, especially for the last strand, will trigger more scholarly attention in language teacher education.

The second up-and-coming research agenda arises from two themes of e-Portfolio-related studies, namely process and application tools. As said, there is no shortage of empirical studies that investigate the effects of e-Portfolio interventions on student affect, including motivation, perceptions, learning engagement and self-regulated learning. These cross-sectional studies usually adopt quasi-experimental or experimental research designs, which cannot reveal the process-orientated aspects of e-Portfolio development. Regarding process, the above review showed that there have not been adequate research insights into students' portfolio keeping experience and students' emotional management when they construct e-Portfolios. To understand e-Portfolio developmental processes, more longitudinal studies are certainly needed to collect trustworthy data. Equally, as pointed out by Bryant and Chittum (2013), professional literature describing the nuts and bolts of various digital software programmes or customised e-Portfolio applications remains scarce. Publications of classroom-based instructional manuals that guide teachers on how to operate common e-Portfolio tools is one highlighted research agenda. This agenda is illustrated again in Chapter 8.

The third agenda that needs attention in e-Portfolio scholarship is likely to be teaching and assessment. Currently, a majority of e-Portfolio-related studies have investigated whether and how the adoption of e-Portfolios at the classroom level has influenced students' learning. For teaching, although there have been numerous action-research studies that described the enablers and barriers of e-Portfolio implementation, little has been done to understand how e-Portfolios can be seamlessly integrated into English language curricula. This agenda is further explored in Chapter 4. As to assessment, scholars are somewhat sceptical about the effectiveness of using e-Portfolios to assess students' language learning summatively. To date, little has been done to understand the validity and reliability of e-Portfolios when they are used as a legitimate classroom-based assessment method. Second, there is no consensus as to which scoring methods or rubrics are the most appropriate for assessing e-Portfolios. Third, owing to the complexity of e-Portfolio contents (i.e. reciprocality, intertextuality, multimodality and spatiality; Yancey, 2004), more research has to be done to understand the effects of focused training in rubric-referenced scoring on teachers'/raters' performances when they grade e-Portfolios.

Summary

Chapter 2 first described different types and aspects of e-Portfolio-related studies. It then discussed three salient elements of e-Portfolio research, namely product, process and tool, followed by a literature review of e-Portfolio scholarship in L2 education in terms of teaching, learning and assessment. The chapter ended with a brief analysis of emerging e-Portfolio research agendas that may enlighten prospective readers who plan to research e-Portfolios.

3 Conceptual Rationale for e-Portfolios

Introduction

Chapter 3 unpacks the conceptual rationale for e-Portfolios in second language (L2) education. The chapter first describes the basic elements, attributes and processes of e-Portfolios. It then discusses three educational theories relating to e-Portfolio use: socio-constructivism, assessment for learning and metacognition. Each of the sub-sections further depicts general ideas, key issues and application challenges behind each theory when they are used to guide e-Portfolio integration. The chapter subsequently evaluates the extent to which the aforementioned theories influence teacher belief and practice in e-Portfolio integration.

Elements, Attributes and Processes

In portfolio scholarship, paper-based portfolios entail four core elements: collection, selection, reflection and deferred evaluation (Burner, 2014). Collection is about student collation of print artefacts in one's portfolio. Selection refers to how students choose their representative works to showcase their best performance. Reflection refers to student engagement in self-reflection on their artefacts. Deferred evaluation refers to grades or marks only assigned to the final submission of paper-based portfolios. These four elements, coupled with self, peer and teacher feedback, are usually presented as a set of iterative activities, which characterise portfolio-based writing instruction (see Figure 3.1). These four elements serve both the formative and summative purposes of assessment concomitantly, although students and teachers tend to pay undue attention to the summative purpose of portfolio assessment, which could diminish the formative benefits of portfolios (Lam & Lee, 2010).

Likewise, e-Portfolios comprise four central elements: creation, revision, curation and circulation, i.e. publication (Yancey, 2019). Creation refers to students' self-generation of artefacts rather than simply uploading artefacts to an e-Portfolio platform. Revision involves students in reworking artefacts upon receipt of multimedia feedback. Curation, via methodical hyperlinking, refers to the organisation of digital artefacts to

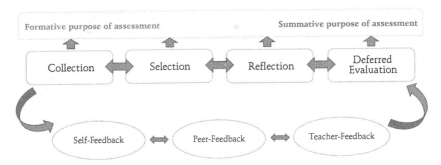

Figure 3.1 Elements of a paper-based portfolio

display students' attainment of subject and digital competence. Circulation is about the display and dissemination of digital artefacts to a target audience, including e-Portfolio design, access and medium of publication (e.g. visual, textual, graphic or audio). Although these four elements are iterative and cyclical, they only serve the formative purpose of assessment since there is no summative assessment component. To increase the validity of e-Portfolios, deferred evaluation could be added as the fifth e-Portfolio element. If process or effort grades are adopted, periodical summative grading in e-Portfolios becomes the best option to balance the formative and summative purposes of assessment (Lam, 2020).

The attributes of e-Portfolios are typically communal, student centred and metacognitive. Since e-Portfolios can be browsed by anyone within a student's community, they promote a community of practice by involving relevant stakeholders in students' e-Portfolio journeys, such as alumni, schoolmates, parents and district educational officers. Corresponding to socio-constructivist ideas, instructional scaffolding among teachers and students and students and students embodies communal practices (Zheng & Barrot, 2022). After all, e-Portfolios are designed for knowledge dissemination and sustainable learning development, which are collective by nature. The attribute of a sense of community further promotes social and collaborative learning, as featured in certain e-Portfolio tasks, namely group digital storytelling and collaborative writing projects. The idea of community is deeply embedded in e-Portfolio-based instruction, since e-Portfolios involve communication with the world, interaction with external stakeholders, negotiation of discourse meanings and the development of one's own digital identity in a new virtual space (Yancey et al., 2013).

The other attribute of e-Portfolios is student centredness. Most e-Portfolio curricula emphasise human agency and autonomy, denoting that students take centre stage in their language learning by mobilising e-Portfolio software tools (Aygün & Aydin, 2016). Since e-Portfolios are highly visible, accessible and transferrable, they support dialogic learning and interactive pedagogies both on- and off-campus effectively, especially during the COVID-19 pandemic. Certain digital platforms and customised e-Portfolio software can facilitate dialogic learning, e.g. the provision of live/pre-recorded audio feedback in the form of screencasts or instantaneous written feedback in the form of web-based interactive word processors. The characteristic of interactivity fits in well with the spirit of assessment for learning, where effective L2 instruction can inform where the student is, where she needs to go and how best she gets there in her learning with teacher input and student motivation for self-monitoring practices (Bennett, 2011).

The last attribute is metacognition, which is a staple activity in portfolio-based instruction. Every portfolio programme, be it paper based or electronic, tends to include reflection. Engaging students in self and peer assessments becomes a signature undertaking in e-Portfolios. Mini self-assessment tasks enable learners to regularly self-reflect on their e-Portfolio artefacts. Peer assessment tasks can enhance students' self-awareness capacity when they apply evaluative judgements to their peers' works as if judging their own. To support metacognition, teachers may emphasise critical thinking, autonomy, self-regulated learning and problem-solving skills as salient features in e-Portfolios (Beckers et al., 2016). When performing self-reflection in e-Portfolios, students are encouraged to set goals, monitor goals, review and adjust learning accordingly. If not doing so, they cannot turn random digital artefacts into valid learning evidence for advancing language development.

E-Portfolio processes characterise synchronisation, integration, multimodality and testimony (Yancey, 2004). Synchronisation refers to teacher and student accessibility to instructional and assessment materials using different digital gadgets. Integration refers to the use of any e-Portfolio platforms that enable students to collate all multimedia and cross-disciplinary artefacts within the same software. Multimodality is about the curation of diverse mediums of artefacts to showcase students' language competency. Testimony refers to how students compile dependable learning evidence to support ongoing language learning via e-Portfolios. These four e-Portfolio processes are elaborated in the following paragraphs.

Synchronisation in e-Portfolio development processes enables quick communication between teachers and students on- and off-campus. Because of the high connectivity of e-Portfolios, students may seek clarifications from more able peers and/or the teacher through forum posts or mobile messaging apps during online lectures whenever misunderstandings arise (Ene & Upton, 2018). Teachers could re-teach a problematic grammar point or explain a cognitively demanding task as observed in the class. This way, e-Portfolio synchronisation facilitates the giving, receiving and enacting of e-feedback on digital or e-Portfolio applications (Chong, 2017). Through the provision of personalised feedback, teachers can cater for learner diversity more effectively. All these instructional remediations might take place in either online or mixed-mode classes. This unique e-Portfolio process further promotes off-campus and flipped learning, especially when students show a strong online presence. Thus, they can become more autonomous in their learning.

Since the e-Portfolio development process is cross-sectoral and longitudinal, it helps students integrate language learning (literacy and oracy skills) and subject learning (major subjects) seamlessly, with the former highlighting skill-based instruction and the latter providing authentic contexts for learning (Eynon & Gambino, 2017). Besides English language, students are encouraged to incorporate other artefacts into their e-Portfolios for curation and reflection owing to the increasing trend of broad-based and lifelong learning. In K-12 settings, teachers across different subject departments may require students to construct one integrative e-Portfolio across grade levels by including mathematics, sciences and experiential learning profiles (i.e. attendance at short-term immersion programmes and co-curricular activities). When students have opportunities to review and showcase interdisciplinary artefacts over time, e-Portfolios open a window for teachers to develop a better understanding of students' whole-person development other than their academic performance.

Multimodality refers to a curating process in e-Portfolios, where students upload multimedia artefacts to intranets, digital or e-Portfolio platforms to showcase their achievements. This process usually promotes creativity, reflective thinking and mastery of technological and language skills, particularly when students create a podcast or a clip on a video-sharing website and link it to their e-Portfolios. The blended use of hyperlinks, websites and social media sites in the e-Portfolio development process enhances students' digital competence skills more than conventional literacy skills. After all, e-Portfolios are a brand-new genre, featuring intertextuality among different modalities of artefacts and reciprocality between e-Portfolio creators and viewers (i.e. negotiations of digital identity; O'Byrne & Murrell, 2014). By way of compiling and curating multimedia artefacts, students find it easier to express themselves, to validate learning evidence and to reach a wider online audienceship.

The processes of creating, referencing and validating learning evidence in e-Portfolios are termed testimony. As e-Portfolios promote evidence-based learning, students are expected to self-reflect on their language learning by presenting relevant evidence with justifications in the form of self-assessments, reflective journal entries or weblog posts (Belgrad, 2013). With regard to e-Portfolio evidence, students are more likely to evaluate their strengths, weaknesses and areas of improvement for future language learning. By so doing, they become more self-conscious of their language development, since learning how to self-reflect on portfolio-based evidence is considered an essential feature of the e-Portfolio compilation process. Because of this, scholars advocate that teachers promulgate a culture of evidence in respective e-Portfolio programmes in order to encourage students to convert submitted artefacts into validated evidence by reflection (via multisource feedback and/or external resources; Lam, 2022c). The following three sections unpack the conceptual rationale for e-Portfolios, including socio-constructivism, assessment for learning and metacognition.

Socio-Constructivism

Principles

According to Vygotsky (1978), a child learning does not occur in a vacuum. In contrast, it takes place with peers or caregivers within a community. Such interactions between one another are a social process that facilitates the acquisition of L2 learning via a Web 2.0 or customised e-Portfolio software. Central to socio-constructivism are the ideas of collaboration, communication and co-construction (Jones & Saville, 2016). These ideas encourage students' active engagement in collective undertakings with peers, teachers and/or parents. In other words, socio-constructivist pedagogies are supposed to be interactive, dialogic and people orientated, given that they support a community of practice, negotiations of identity development and the co-construction of new knowledge/discourses by way of respective e-Portfolio platforms, be they blogging systems, social media or institutional intranets (Roy & Putatunda, 2020). Likewise, the socio-constructivist approach to L2 learning entails peer learning, student engagement, self and peer assessments, collaborative learning and motivation (Kelly, 2018). Since these socio-constructivist characteristics are primarily student centred and socially situated, teachers assume the role of facilitator rather than instructor, providing students with timely and staged scaffolding whenever necessary. Students' classmates also have a role to play by providing peer support for one another. Therefore, socio-constructivism is likely to foster dialogic pedagogy and deep learning, in which students are placed at the centre of e-Portfolio-based classrooms (Wang & Lee, 2021).

One of the most prominent principles of socio-constructivism is the zone of proximal development (ZPD), emphasising that a child succeeds in learning a language by interacting with a more capable other (i.e. their peers, teacher or parents), and by interacting with a digital environment (i.e. e-Portfolio contents and online resources; Bozkurt, 2017). During this dynamic learning process, the more capable others and external digital environments serve as a scaffold to facilitate the child's L2 acquisition. In the socio-constructivist theory, the ZPD and scaffolding always go hand in hand. Scaffolded instruction is generally delivered in the following sequence: explicit instruction (by teachers, also more knowledgeable others), shared demonstration and guided practice (among teachers and students) and independent practice (by students only). Within an e-Portfolio platform, electronic scaffolding occurs in the first two instructional phases to support the child's learning, because mediatory artefacts (i.e. the child's representative work with peer and teacher feedback) can bring her to the next level of learning. In the ZPD, language learning occurs by way of interaction, negotiation and collaboration in a virtual communal space, namely synchronous or asynchronous conversations on an e-Portfolio platform. These dialogues facilitate parts of children's cognitive development and the co-construction of new knowledge for their e-Portfolio contents through mini group projects, collaborative writing, problem-solving tasks or individual tasks requiring deep thinking (Lam et al., 2023). Furthermore, the ZPD lays the foundation for dialogic learning, since ongoing exchanges throughout the e-Portfolio compilation process are likely to empower children to create new meanings and new discourse in their L2 development (Yancey, 2009).

Classroom examples

Self and peer assessment tasks are the most common examples to demonstrate the classroom application of socio-constructivism. Since one salient e-Portfolio attribute is metacognition, the inclusion of self and peer assessments as part of instructional events can perhaps enhance students' metacognitive capacity in the long run, not to mention the uptake of learning-how-to-learn study skills progressively (Li, 2017). Collaborative writing is another typical e-Portfolio activity, which reflects the essence of socio-constructivism. Students can participate in synchronous group writing projects via web-based word processors (e.g. Google Docs) or hypertextual publication tools (e.g. wiki), which are in sync with most e-Portfolio platforms (Lam et al., 2023). In collaborative writing, students can engage in dialogic learning naturally, because learning through online self and peer editing becomes a regular feature of most e-Portfolio programmes, especially when students are off-campus (Li & Zhang, 2021; Li et al., 2022). Helping students to produce multimedia e-Portfolio artefacts by internalising success criteria or exemplars is likely to promote the socio-constructivist approach to learning, given that this type of inductive instructional design requires students to discern the key features of quality work by means of ongoing interaction, negotiation and exploration throughout the e-Portfolio compilation process (Lam, 2019). Staged scaffolding in the form of virtual dialogues (chatbot, chatbox or forum posts) provides more opportunities for students to learn from the teacher, artificial intelligence (AI)-powered software (Lee, 2023), as well as key opinion leaders of public speaking (i.e. tutorial clips about proper English pronunciation on YouTube). It also creates a positive and supportive online environment for students and teachers to co-participate in a community of practice (Russell & Murphy-Judy, 2021).

Implementation challenges

Although socio-constructivism promotes peer learning and reflective thinking in L2 curricula, its classroom implementation is not without challenges, particularly when teachers and students experience unexpected technical and pedagogical obstacles using any digital or e-Portfolio applications. For instance, Aydin (2014) discovered that the study's student informants could enhance their literacy and research skills when using Facebook-based e-Portfolios. However, the informants found it difficult to revise their interim drafts and give feedback to coursemates on the software interface. Zheng and Barrot (2022) reported that after using a social media-based e-Portfolio application, i.e. QQ, the informants' speaking performance improved moderately although they encountered a plethora of technical (e.g. internet connection) and learning-related challenges (e.g. the appropriateness of QQ as a platform). Likewise, Kelly (2018) found that the socio-constructivist approach to teaching an L2 (via Facebook) could improve university-level informants' linguistic competence, namely their receptive and vocabulary skills. Nevertheless, some of the informants preferred not to adopt Facebook as a learning site because the social networking platform was likely to distract their language learning and should be used for social rather than academic purposes. In design education, Charles (2022) observed that socio-constructivist instructional approaches such as one-on-one tutorials, small-group tutorials and design reviews (crits) might not survive a smooth transition from an in-person to a virtual learning environment, since the dynamic features of dialogic and collaborative learning were likely to be diminished due to an apparent lack of face-to-face interactions as in the physical studio.

Assessment for Learning

Definitions

Like other educational approaches, assessment for learning has numerous definitions. Since its inception in the late 1990s, assessment for learning has undergone conceptual transformations. Thus far, at least two generations of definition have emerged – the first in 2002 and the second in 2009. In 2002, the Assessment Reform Group published an oft-cited definition of assessment for learning:

> Assessment for Learning is the process of seeking and interpreting evidence for use by learners and their teachers to decide where the learners are in their learning, where they need to go and how best to get there. (Assessment Reform Group, 2002: 2–3)

The first-generation definition emphasises the use of appropriate assessment information to fine-tune the teaching and learning process in order to close students' learning gaps. This definition is underpinned by the idea of formative assessment, where learners and teachers reflect upon, interpret and enact assessment data to regulate learning (Bennett, 2011). In other words, this version of the definition focuses on active learner agency and self-reflective process. Almost a decade later, owing to constant misinterpretations of the assessment for learning principles and the distortion of its classroom applications, some assessment scholars, especially those from the Asia-Pacific region, advocated an updated version of the definition backed by socio-constructivist and learner-centred theories (Swaffield, 2011). This second-generation definition was a by-product of the Third International Conference on Assessment for Learning held in Dunedin, New Zealand, in 2009. It stated:

> Assessment for Learning is part of everyday practice by students, teachers, and peers that seeks, reflects upon and responds to information from dialogue, demonstration and observation in ways that enhance ongoing learning. (Klenowski, 2009: 264)

The second-generation definition highlights the more immediate impact of dynamic pedagogies on student learning. Although initiated by teachers, assessment for learning remains student centred and is considered an enquiry-based learning process (Black, 2015). Assessment information gathered from dialogue, demonstration and observation is largely formative, qualitative and contingent, which provides students with timely input on how to improve future works. This latest definition is all-embracing, involving an overhaul of instructional approaches, curriculum planning and wider educational policy. The definition is also a natural response to scholars' request for theorising assessment for learning when used as a classroom-based assessment practice. In view of this, Black and Wiliam (2009) further elaborated on five aspects of formative assessment:

1. Clarifying and sharing learning intentions and criteria for success;
2. Engineering effective classroom discussions and other learning tasks that elicit evidence of student understanding;
3. Providing feedback that moves learners forward;
4. Activating students as instructional resources for one another; and
5. Activating students as the owners of their own learning. (Black & Wiliam, 2009: 8)

Apparently, these five assessment for learning aspects dovetail with the essence of the second-generation definition, given that teachers take up the role of critical commentators and students assume the role of autonomous learners in the constructivist instructional process (Lam, 2018c).

Debates

Although assessment for learning has been adopted in general and language education for over two decades, teachers and scholars remain confused about the distinctions between this term and formative assessment. Debates arise regarding whether these two concepts are synonymous or different, and how they are dissimilar if the latter is true. In the assessment literature, certain scholars have used the two terms interchangeably or even equivalently, whereas some have stated that formative assessment and assessment for learning are different (cf. Bennett, 2011). They notice that formative assessment is generally considered constructive feedback that supports learning, while assessment for learning is one prominent pedagogical approach to formative assessment. Swaffield (2011) has listed six discrepancies between formative assessment and assessment for learning. First, assessment for learning is about good teaching and learning, whereas formative assessment is a purpose of assessment. Second, assessment for learning is somewhat immediate, whereas formative assessment usually occurs over a longer timeframe. Third, assessment for learning is more context specific influencing particular groups of students and teachers, whereas formative assessment involves more stakeholders and is extensive in scope. Fourth, assessment for learning emphasises learner agency and autonomy, whereas formative assessment permits learners to be passive. Fifth, assessment for learning is a learning process itself, whereas formative assessment provides useful information to guide students on how to improve future learning. Sixth, assessment for learning is about learning how to learn in one's own learning journey, whereas formative assessment is linked to specific curricular goals. Although these six discrepancies appear to be contentious when manifested in various educational contexts, the distinctions between assessment for learning and formative assessment remain evident (Wiliam, 2011). For instance, assessment for learning primarily promotes learning-how-to-learn skills, whereas formative assessment could support student uptake of self- and co-regulated learning skills via teacher-led scaffolding, such as explicit instruction and teacher feedback (Gu & Lam, 2023). Similarly, assessment for learning is considered an effective instructional approach, while formative assessment is regarded as an assessment purpose among many others, including summative, diagnostic and evaluative purposes of assessment (Black & Wiliam, 2009).

Relevance to e-Portfolios

Sharing success criteria with students, having dialogues about learning improvement, providing revisable feedback and engaging students in self and peer assessments are the basics of assessment for learning as well as key features of e-Portfolios, especially when students are encouraged to frequently exchange e-Portfolio contents and critically reflect upon digital artefacts with multisource e-feedback, i.e. dialogic and collaborative learning (Lam *et al.*, 2023). Along with formal virtual lectures and informal online chats, some customised e-Portfolio platforms can facilitate teacher–student interactions both inside and outside the school campus, e.g. Seesaw and Schoology. More details about various digital and e-Portfolio tools are discussed in Chapter 8. Assessment for learning is underpinned by learner-centred pedagogies, as are e-Portfolios. Students are expected to be the owner and creator of their own e-Portfolios. In other words, they create, revise, curate and disseminate their e-Portfolio artefacts to achieve the learning-orientated assessment purpose. These defining features of e-Portfolios are said to be ideal for materialising 'authentic' assessment for learning, which is formative and emphasises the dynamism between students and teachers (Lam, 2020; Swaffield, 2011). Another commonality between assessment for learning and e-Portfolios is their ultimate goal to help students become self-evaluative in their current learning and beyond (Li & Li, 2022). Through learning-how-to-learn strategies in assessment for learning and self-reflection in e-Portfolios, students can engage in reviewing, monitoring and modifying artefacts as valid evidence to improve future language learning, namely writing (Skar *et al.*, 2022). Such a metacognitive attribute is unique in assessment for learning and e-Portfolios.

Metacognition

Components and applications

Metacognition refers to thinking about thinking. It has three key components, comprising knowledge (cognition of target language), skills (adoption of learning strategies) and attitudes (motivational beliefs) to support how learners acquire an L2 academically (Fukuda *et al.*, 2022). The tripartite components enable learners to plan, monitor and evaluate the extent to which they have mastered the target language. Near the turn of the century, metacognition became high on educational reform agendas owing to the fact that the idea of learning-how-to-learn has been globally recognised as one of the most significant 21st-century study skills (Carless, 2017). Additionally, ministries of education in many parts of the world have advocated the core value of lifelong learning in their curricula, which could be implemented through assessment for learning practices as described in the previous section. One common classroom application of metacognition is assessment as learning, which is a subset of assessment for learning (Earl, 2013). Assessment as learning is defined as one form of authentic assessment that encourages students to be dynamic, committed and critical assessors who make sense of incoming information, relate it to prior knowledge and create new learning metacognitively (Earl & Katz, 2008). In L2 classrooms, assessment as learning could be used for pre-writing (goal setting), during writing (monitoring via self-assessing) and post-writing activities (revising with feedback) to enhance students' metacognitive capacities (Lee *et al.*, 2019).

Self- and co-regulated learning

Metacognition is one key aspect of self-regulated learning, alongside students' cognition, social behaviours and motivational regulation (Teng, 2022). The construct of self-regulated learning is underpinned by the principles of formative assessment, where students exercise active agency to close their learning gaps by utilising a range of cognitive and metacognitive strategies with regard to multimodal feedback (Clark, 2012). In their oft-cited definition, Pintrich and Zusho (2002: 64) considered self-regulated learning 'an active constructive process whereby learners set goals for their learning and monitor, regulate, and control their cognition, motivation, and behaviour, guided and constrained by their goals and the contextual features of the environment'. According to Zimmerman's (2002) model, self-regulated learning has three phases: forethought, performance and self-reflection. In the forethought phase, students set goals, analyse tasks and plan pertinent activities. In the performance phase, they monitor learning and adopt effective strategies to achieve the goals. In the self-reflection phase, they self-assess their learning critically and make adjustments whenever necessary. Of these three phases, the performance phase constitutes a core component of formative assessment, which serves to scaffold students to acquire their self-regulated learning skills. In fact, self-regulated language learning bears a resemblance to essential formative assessment practices, e.g. goal planning, goal setting, monitoring and reviewing (Andrade, 2019).

Self-regulated learning is mainly concerned with internal processes, engaging students in regulating the cognitive, metacognitive and motivational aspects of language learning. Although self-regulated learning emphasises the individual learner, Zimmerman's (2002) self-regulated learning was formulated based upon a social cognitive model. Thus, in e-Portfolios, students are supposed to partake in the co-regulation of learning, indicating that they interact with (more capable) peers, teachers, caregivers and an immediate social environment (Hadwin *et al.*, 2018). Some scholars claim that co-regulated learning involves not only 'the joint influence on student learning of the learner's processes of self-regulation but also of the sources of regulation in the learning environment' (Allal, 2020: 338). These sources of regulation include school curricula, instructional materials, teacher pedagogical approaches, assessment methods and technological tools. In other words, co-regulation of learning appears to make more sense in e-Portfolio curricula, because e-Portfolios characterise collaborative learning, community of practice and online dissemination of e-Portfolio contents. All these features represent the interaction and its regulatory process between the student and their immediate context in a portfolio community (Chen & Bonner, 2020). That said, self-regulated learning remains a core component in e-Portfolios, given that students need to self-assess, self-monitor and self-reflect before they can compile their digital artefacts. Allal (2020) has argued that self-regulated and co-regulated learning coexist rather than substituting one another. Instead, self-regulated learning supports co-regulated learning processes in conjunction with the contextual sources of regulation to enhance L2 learning to the full.

Feedback and metacognition

Feedback plays a crucial role in paper-based and electronic portfolios. It is a catalyst to assist students to bridge the gaps between their current and expected levels of learning performance, namely in portfolio assessment of writing (Lam, 2015a). Traditionally, feedback is viewed as one-way information, passing from the teacher to students. Therefore, it is less likely that students will adopt, internalise and reuse this kind of feedback, especially when teacher feedback is perceived as illegible, incomprehensible or non-actionable (Lam, 2017a). In the last decade, assessment scholars have proven that effective feedback is expected to be process orientated, dialogic and sustainable, so that students can actively engage in the feedback process to improve their L2 learning and teachers can generate constructive feedback as one form of professional development to enhance their feedback literacy (Lee, 2021b). Furthermore, these scholars have claimed that feedback involving technology, e.g. the use of synchronous audio feedback in e-Portfolios, is probable to create favourable virtual conditions for students to engage in feedback dialogues (i.e. online self and peer assessments) and the uptake of multimodal feedback for future learning (i.e. sustained e-feedback for knowledge transfer; Carless & Winstone, 2020).

In feedback scholarship, academics have long associated the effectiveness of feedback with its self-regulatory function. To harness the usefulness of feedback, teachers can empower students to regulate received feedback information and encourage them to foster self-evaluative judgements during the portfolio process. Hattie and Timperley (2007) formulated a feedback model composed of three questions and four dimensions of feedback that helped students to close their learning gaps. The three questions are: Where am I going? How am I going? and Where to next? They are operated under the four types of feedback: task, process, self-regulation and self. Their review study showed that process- and self-regulated-related feedback were most effective, as students were expected to think about how to improve their work relating to success criteria and self-set goals, respectively. These two feedback types also promote student reflective thinking in an iterative feedback process, so that students can become more critical, evaluative and self-regulating. Adopting Hattie and Timperley's model, Lam (2015a, 2015b) discovered that university-level student informants were able to revise their interim drafts more accurately after they were given process- and self-regulated-related feedback. They had more opportunities to upgrade their works in progress independent of the teacher.

Teacher Belief and Practice of e-Portfolio Integration

By and large, e-Portfolios are communal (a feature of socio-constructivism), interactive (an aspect of assessment for learning) and reflective (a facet of metacognition). In the past 20 years, teachers from different educational contexts have been trying out diverse versions of e-Portfolio instruction and assessment practices underpinned by socio-constructivist, assessment for learning and self-regulated learning principles. Nevertheless, scholars have reported that most assessment for learning principles were misinterpreted by teachers and their pertinent classroom practices were unavoidably distorted (Black & Wiliam, 2018). Such conceptual misunderstanding is constrained by a plethora of individual, institutional and contextual factors. For instance, teachers' lukewarm change in belief and practice was bound by limited initial professional training in e-learning (Bowman *et al.*, 2016). Some teachers reluctantly introduced a weak version of paper-based or electronic portfolios owing to a conservative school culture in the Asia-Pacific region (Lam *et al.*, 2023). Oftentimes, the application of formative e-Portfolio programmes is restricted by a larger exam-driven culture, which turns assessment for learning practices into exam preparation tutorials or additional after-school lessons (Winstone & Carless, 2019). In fact, in two special issues of *Assessment in Education: Principles, Policy & Practice* published in 2009 and 2015, both guest editors pinpointed the caveats of adopting an instrumental approach to delivering formative assessment as it would diminish its learning potentials, such as dialogic learning, and exacerbate the teaching-to-the-test practice, such as exam-focused drillings (Black, 2015; Klenowski, 2009). If teachers implement their e-Portfolio programmes with low fidelity, these programmes may become a top-down, teacher-centred and procedural compliant model, which runs counter to the conceptual rationale for e-Portfolios. As stated by Black (2015), any educational innovations, such as e-Portfolio integration into L2 contexts, may take two years (or more) to witness an apparent change in teacher belief and practice.

Summary

Chapter 3 unpacked the conceptual rationale for e-Portfolios. First, it revealed e-Portfolio elements (e.g. collection, selection and reflection), attributes (e.g. a community of practice and metacognition) and processes (e.g. synchronisation and multimodality). The chapter then discussed three major educational theories that underpin e-Portfolio integration in L2 classrooms, including socio-constructivism, assessment for learning and metacognition. The definitions, conceptual debates, applications and implementation challenges of each theory were addressed. Finally, Chapter 3 discussed teacher belief and practice of e-Portfolio integration.

4 E-Portfolios for Curriculum Planning and Teaching

Introduction

Chapter 4 discusses how teachers plan, design and implement e-Portfolio curricula in second language (L2) classrooms. First, the chapter describes features and elements of e-Portfolio curricula in first language (L1) and L2 contexts. It then introduces the teaching of four language skills in typical e-Portfolio programmes, namely listening, speaking, reading and writing. Afterwards, three approaches to e-Portfolio integration into English curricula are elucidated, followed by an evaluation of their pros and cons. The last section presents procedural guidelines on how to plan and design e-Portfolio curricula based upon tried-and-tested digital language curriculum models.

Features and Elements of e-Portfolio Curricula

This section describes the essential features and elements of e-Portfolio-based curricula in L2 contexts. As mentioned in Chapter 3, e-Portfolio compilation processes comprise creation, curation, revision and circulation (dissemination), which are typically characterised as exploratory, metacognitive and communal (Yancey, 2019). With these major features in mind, e-Portfolio curricula are expected to be *inquiry based*, *reflective* and *collaborative* in nature, since learners take centre stage in L2 instruction (Li & Li, 2022). To be inquiry based, the design of e-Portfolio curricula is supposed to be analytical, problem-solving and experiential, so that students can develop adequate strategic competence to acquire a second or a foreign language (Aygün & Aydin, 2016). To be reflective, e-Portfolio tasks should include reflective practices that encourage students to self-assess and self-reflect on their works in progress regularly throughout a designated instructional period (Mazloomi & Khabiri, 2018). To be collaborative, e-Portfolio learning activities are designed to involve peers, teachers, parents and external members as co-participants to establish a joint venture and foster a sense of shared ownership (Lam, 2022a).

In e-Portfolio curricula, *creation* encapsulates the feature of inquiry based pedagogy. It allows students to compose multimedia artefacts and to showcase their language learning. In addition to fulfilling the coursework requirements, students have autonomy in making decisions as to what genre, rhetoric, format and medium of artefacts are created. In the creation process, students may practice research and problem-solving skills when they compose a novel genre or investigate a topical issue. *Curation* involves a two-step procedure, in which students select which artefacts best represent their language abilities and then organise these artefacts as a coherent whole in e-Portfolios. Selecting and organising artefacts require students to continuously perform self-reflection. Upon receipt of e-feedback, students revise and upgrade their artefacts in accordance with their learning goals. *Revision*, in fact, occurs throughout the e-Portfolio compilation process. Curation and revision dovetail with the reflective feature of e-Portfolio curricula. *Circulation* refers to how students upload, convert and relocate artefacts within their own e-Portfolio console before they share the portfolio contents with the public online. Circulation captures the collaborative attribute of e-Portfolio curricula since students usually disseminate their work to a wider virtual community.

The elements of e-Portfolio curricula are conceptually derived from three phenomena in language education (Eynon & Gambino, 2017). First, owing to the rise of learner-centred and socio-constructivist pedagogies, the adoption of technology in L2 education enables students and teachers to engage in self-reflective and lifelong learning more readily (Belgrad, 2013). Second, the advent of Web 2.0 applications and the internet around the turn of the century facilitated technology in integrating learning across educational levels, subject disciplines, languages and cultures (Light *et al.*, 2012). Third, discontent with conventional norm-referenced and discrete-point assessments, teachers and scholars have started a new movement to advance authentic assessment practices, namely from selected-response tests to constructed-response assessments (Abrar-ul-Hassan *et al.*, 2021). The aforementioned contextual factors have accelerated the development of an alternative pedagogical paradigm that utilises digital technology to connect three central elements of e-Portfolio curricula, namely (a) reflective learning, (b) integrative pedagogy and (c) authentic assessment. These three elements are further explained below. The presence of these elements in e-Portfolio curricula may vary depending on which educational agendas are prioritised. For instance, self-reflective practices may not be emphasised in certain teacher-led curricula, while integrative pedagogy remains impractical when subject teachers prefer working in isolation.

Reflective learning is one key element in e-Portfolio curricula. E-Portfolios are said to provide abundant opportunities for students to engage in reflective practices when they are learning an L2. These reflective practices may need to be guided by more capable others, namely advanced peers or teachers, as reflection for language enhancement is a complex undertaking (Lam *et al.*, 2023). Reflective learning in e-Portfolio curricula can promulgate sustainable learning because students should train to be independent of teacher scaffolding after formal schooling. Concerning integrative pedagogy, e-Portfolio curricula help students to connect past, current and future learning events holistically. The integrative element supports the transfer of multidisciplinary knowledge, the development of intercultural competence, as well as mastery of social learning through collective meaning-making processes (Cummins & Davesne, 2009). Not only does integrative pedagogy promote life-wide learning, but it also warrants a longitudinal and developmental approach to L2 learning across time, knowledge, experience and emotions in a balanced manner. The trend of adopting e-Portfolios as authentic assessment in face-to-face and remote teaching has become indispensable. The making of e-Portfolio artefacts simulates the creation of authentic language tasks, e.g. audio-recording a podcast or setting up a personal website. Teachers may treat these learning tasks as authentic assessment tasks to increase the content and construct validity of e-Portfolio assessment (Green, 2022). Authentic assessment in e-Portfolio curricula aligns with students' learning of writing, because students' learning and assessing of writing occur concomitantly (Lam, 2021b). Learning to assess in e-Portfolio curricula is also beneficial to students' development of lifelong learning. The next section discusses the teaching of four language skills in an e-Portfolio programme.

Teaching of Four Skills in e-Portfolio Programmes

The teaching of the four skills in L2 instruction refers to listening, speaking, reading and writing. Listening and reading skills are called receptive skills, whereas speaking and writing are called productive skills. In English language teaching, scholars have debated whether the four skills are taught in an integrated or an isolated approach in order to enhance their effectiveness (Hinkel, 2006). Apparently, there are pros and cons to either approach. For the pros, adopting the integrated approach mirrors the authenticity and validity of language learning and daily communications since the holistic use of the four skills is fundamental to students' L2 acquisition. For the cons, students are less likely to master the four skills equally proficiently, especially for certain L2 learners who perform better in receptive skills than in productive skills (Burns & Siegel, 2018). The pros of utilising the isolated approach are relatively focused for students, so that teachers can more easily identify their weakness in one language skill. The cons are that this approach is not contextualised and runs counter to the contemporary instructional approach, namely task-based language teaching that promulgates the dynamic use of the four skills to complete learning tasks (Harmer, 2015).

In the following, although the characteristics of the four skills and their instructional ideas are presented consecutively, the teaching of the four skills remains integrated within an e-Portfolio curriculum. Listening instruction involves teaching top-down and bottom-up processing skills. The top-down processing skills refer to students' use of global and contextual knowledge to predict and interpret what they hear. The bottom-up processing skills refer to students' focus on the details of connected speech, namely phonemes, morphemes, sound–word mapping among other aspects. Linguists identified that some L2 learners lacked lexical, grammatical and contextual knowledge or strategic competence (e.g. requests for repetitions) when they listen (Yin, 2022). These learners need training in acquiring top-down and bottom-up listening skills. Thus, scholars have suggested adopting a 'comprehensive' approach to teaching listening, such as two-way listening as in Zoom interviews (Goh & Vandergrift, 2021). In e-Portfolios, teachers may select age-appropriate podcasts as input and construct open-ended listening tasks to promote extensive listening. Alternatively, teachers can adapt video clips by editing those uploaded on video hosting sites, e.g. YouTube, as authentic listening material. With images, audios and subtitles, students may find it motivating to complete those tasks, which could link to writing (composing of a post-listening written summary in forums) and speaking (oral response to a topical event in audio files) practices.

Speaking instruction comprises the teaching of language systems, discourse knowledge and the core skills of speech production, namely conceptualisation, formulation, articulation and self-monitoring. It entails developing students' speaking competence, e.g. speech rate, intelligibility, turn-taking and repairment of breakdowns (Thornbury, 2012). Although most speaking instructional methods emphasise interactions and negotiations of meanings, they usually lack providing students with adequate scaffolding, such as offering guided input and planning for students, raising students' awareness of their speech production via reflection and providing timely feedback for students to improve intelligibility (Goh & Burns, 2012). To this end, e-Portfolios can create a supportive environment for students to master speaking skills. Screencasting, hyperlinked to e-Portfolios, is an option because students need to draft a script, create screencasts, prepare voiceovers and edit videos and audios for their presentations (Renwick, 2017). Teachers may invite students to create screencasts on how to augment students' vocabulary power by demonstrating the use of antonyms, synonyms, hyponyms and polysemy with animations and annotations. Students are encouraged to perform self and peer assessments on their screencasts to improve their tone, pace, intonation and pronunciation accordingly. With these formative assessment practices, students can raise their metalinguistic awareness and reflect upon their speaking competence (Zheng & Barrot, 2022).

Reading instruction is about the teaching of high-level and low-level processing skills in decoding written texts. The former comprises use of cognitive/metacognitive reading strategies and resources for comprehension, whereas the latter consists of word recognition, lexico-syntactic and semantic processing skills (Sadeghi, 2021). Since reading abilities have a strong correlation with academic success, teachers typically place a premium on reading instruction (Nation, 2009). Print-to-speech instruction such as reading aloud word by word or choral reading of short sentences could be robotic and unmotivated whereas online reading instruction is likely to promote enjoyment and participation. Engaging students in browsing multimedia texts (i.e. graphics, videos, audios, hyperlinks and social media sites) via mobile apps (e.g. ReadEra) or e-readers (e.g. Kindle) has become an upward trend (Kang et al., 2021). Before class, teachers can assign students to read a passage uploaded onto the e-Portfolio platform. Students are trained to adopt a range of online reading strategies, including e-dictionaries, translation apps and pronunciation tutorials to practice intensive reading. To practice extensive reading, teachers encourage students to read a longer text, namely a novel, over time, to take notes by utilising the annotation features of an e-reader and then to draft a book report based on these annotations.

Writing instruction refers to the teaching of linguistic, textual and sociocultural knowledge plus cognitive and metacognitive composing strategies. There are three popular writing instructional approaches: product-based instruction (the text), process writing instruction (the writer) and genre-based instruction (audience and context; for details, cf. Li, 2017). Owing to the ever-changing L2 writing landscape, an eclectic model, named the 'process-genre' approach, came to prominence to embrace students' development of cognitive composing skills and sociocultural knowledge about topics, audience and cultural norms concurrently (Hyland, 2021). Despite this new model, the increasing trend of technological use in writing instruction suggests an overhaul of current L2 writing pedagogies, e.g. a shift from paper-based to electronic portfolios (Lam, 2021b). Using Web 2.0 applications as e-Portfolio platforms is common because learning management systems, social networking sites, weblogs and open-source commercial software have been used in many e-Portfolio-based programmes. Teachers may adopt these applications to engage students in collaborative writing tasks (digital storytelling; Cheung, 2022). They could encourage students to practice peer response on blogging sites and Facebook-based portfolios in order to improve both composing and peer feedback skills (Nicolaidou, 2013). Teachers should also emphasise the role of self-reflection when students curate their digital artefacts. The next section describes three approaches to integrating e-Portfolios into English curricula.

E-Portfolio Integration into English Curricula

To integrate e-Portfolios into English curricula, teachers may consider three options: a blended approach, a provisional approach and a personal approach (Lam, 2019). A blended approach is to integrate e-Portfolio applications into the current English curriculum. Compiling, curating and reflecting upon learning through multimedia artefacts become part of the programme learning outcomes and will be summatively evaluated near the end of a school term/year. The advantages of this approach are fourfold. Teachers have sufficient time to plan, design and evaluate e-Portfolio tasks in connection with the teaching of the four skills and grammar. Using this approach, e-Portfolio integration could also enhance teachers' language assessment literacy since they need to acquire pertinent knowledge and skills in revamping e-Portfolio-based curricula. Students are likely to be more motivated to participate in e-Portfolio compilation if e-Portfolios are legitimatised as formal L2 learning. Parents and students can understand the purposes of e-Portfolio instruction at the start of a course, as these are required coursework components. The major drawback of this approach is that teachers are perhaps overloaded by giving students e-Portfolio training alongside daily language teaching, given that instructional hours remain the same. After all, students may need additional scaffolding in mastering e-Portfolio development processes if it is their first time experiencing this instructional approach.

A provisional approach refers to e-Portfolio integration as a one-off measure rather than a regular feature of L2 curricula. In this approach, e-Portfolio integration takes the form of add-on components, lasting for a shorter duration, namely from a writing cycle to one semester. Teachers may be less involved in systematic curriculum planning and integration processes as compared to the first approach because e-Portfolio is an option. Additionally, the provisional approach, when introduced in L2 classroom contexts, could be informal, flexible and not labour intensive provided that teachers only require students to compile their existing homework assignments, namely notes, quizzes, interim drafts and projects, and convert them into digital artefacts for curation and reflection. In terms of workload, teachers and students feel less pressurised since they regard e-Portfolios as a digital platform to take stock of language instruction unofficially. Nevertheless, owing to its short-lived nature, students may not take e-Portfolio learning seriously, especially when they realise that their e-Portfolios are not graded (Lam, 2020). This approach is predominantly appropriate for teachers who want to get hands-on experience to pilot e-Portfolios for the first time and see whether this instructional approach could be properly incorporated into their curriculum.

A personal approach alludes to students' e-Portfolio keeping as a learning companion throughout their schooling. Personalised e-Portfolios are neither standardised in format nor institutionalised in content, since students can freely set learning goals, decide what artefacts to upload and review the best artefacts that represent their language learning trajectories. Broadly speaking, this approach empowers students to be independent, reflective and critical by taking charge of their learning with e-Portfolios continuously. In addition to the initial start-up in each key learning stage (i.e. Grades 4, 7 and 10), students are encouraged to compile interdisciplinary artefacts across grade levels and showcase their best academic performance via multimodal artefacts to potential admission officers or future employers. Despite being autonomous, teachers need to provide early intervention regarding what Web 2.0 tools students and parents should select, what artefacts they should compile and how they technically organise and review artefacts on those platforms. Teachers at different educational levels may communicate with one another in order to provide moral and/or academic support to students whenever necessary, although this additional assistance should be kept to a minimum. If students adopt this e-Portfolio approach, they need to be committed to their L2 learning.

This paragraph describes three types of e-Portfolio programmes and discusses the extent to which they could be integrated into conventional product-based, textbook-bound English curricula. Full details of the three portfolio-based programmes were reported in Lam (2019: 13). They include the whole-language portfolio, reading-and-writing portfolio and interdisciplinary portfolio programmes. First, the whole-language portfolio programme involves the teaching of the four language skills holistically. It helps students master L2 learning through a communicative approach. Since the nature of the programme is skill based and contextualised, its compatibility with existing curricula remains high. Teachers may integrate the whole-language e-Portfolio programme into curricula using the *blended* approach because it may take teachers more preparation time to launch this programme in context. Second, the reading-and-writing portfolio programme underscores literacy instruction. It enhances L2 learners' literacy skills. As the programme features process writing, appreciation of literary texts and metacognitive awareness raising, it fits in well with some process-orientated and collaborative L2 writing classrooms. Teachers may integrate this e-Portfolio programme into curricula using the *provisional* approach because this approach is flexible and involves less preparation if literacy instruction is already prioritised. Third, the interdisciplinary portfolio programme advocates personalised learning. It targets developing students' mastery of life-wide learning and knowledge transfer skills. Because the programme is broad in scope and difficult to coordinate, its compatibility with the existing curriculum is somewhat low. Teachers may train students to adopt e-Portfolios as a learning companion using the *personal* approach unless schools are willing to formally take up this broad spectrum project. The following section discusses procedural guidelines on how teachers can plan and design their e-Portfolio curricula.

Procedural Guidelines on Planning and Designing e-Portfolio Curricula

Thus far, there has been a plethora of language curriculum frameworks that guide teachers to design their school-based English curricula. Of these, the common components consist of initial planning (setting of objectives), content selection, methodology and course/ programme evaluation (cf. Nunan, 2012; Richards, 2013). Meanwhile, theorists and researchers have published similar scholarship regarding how teachers can plan, design and develop their writing portfolio and/ or portfolio assessment programmes in L1 and L2 contexts (cf. Lam, 2018a, 2019; Moya & O'Malley, 2001). The prototype of a portfolio-based curriculum framework for English as a foreign language (EFL) learners originated from Delett et al.'s (2001: 60) model, which entailed seven components: (1) set assessment purpose; (2) identify instructional objectives; (2a) match tasks to objectives; (2b) set assessment criteria; (3) determine organisation; (4) monitor progress; and (5) evaluate the overall portfolio process. These seven aspects dovetail well with the objective–content–methodology–evaluation components of generic English language curriculum frameworks with two additional elements: organisation of portfolio layouts, medium and artefacts; and how portfolio-based instruction is being monitored.

Regardless of these frameworks, they were designed for face-to-face instruction and not for online teaching. Since 2000, a number of online instructional design models have emerged in response to ever-increasing e-learning demands in L2 education (Alonso et al., 2005). Of these models, their common components include (a) preparation, (b) concepts of design, (c) teaching online and (d) learning outcomes and evaluation (Luić, 2020). The major divergence between in-person and remote language curriculum frameworks is that the latter involve more preparation time, since online instructional approaches, communication patterns and e-assessment practices are novel to teachers and students alike in certain L2 contexts. Teachers, perhaps, need extra professional development training and technical support, as do their students. They may want to learn how to locate online course materials, to upload/download assignments and to receive e-feedback. Facilitating student–student, student–teacher and student–technology communications in e-Portfolio platforms is another pedagogical consideration in online language curriculum planning because authentic interactions are unquestionably sacrificed due to class suspensions, city lockdowns or home quarantine restrictions (Gacs et al., 2020).

In her recent work, Luić (2020: 6453) rigorously reviewed a number of traditional and digital curriculum designs. She subsequently created a conceptual model of curriculum convergence, which entails four key components: (i) learning outcomes, (ii) methodology, (iii) communication patterns and (iv) assessment (see Figure 4.1). *Learning outcomes* include needs analysis, course description, debriefing of learning outcomes and assessment criteria. *Methodology* is about types of instruction, synchronicity and teaching schedule. *Communication patterns* refer to modes of interaction, feedback channels, types of learning tasks and technical support. *Assessment* alludes to timeframe, frequency of formative and summative assessments, and participation in online forums, discussion groups or pertinent project-based assignments. Although this quadripartite curriculum model was developed based upon traditional curriculum models, it has two features that warrant effective online teaching and learning. One is (ii) methodology, which offers different types of virtual instruction and modes of delivery. Another is (iii) communication patterns, which utilise various forms of virtual classroom interactions to substitute for face-to-face interactions when remote teaching takes place.

The following paragraphs delineate the four-step online instructional design guidelines to assist teachers in planning and developing e-Portfolio

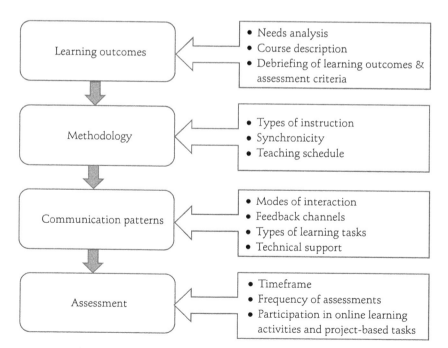

Figure 4.1 A model of an e-Portfolio curriculum (adapted from Luić, 2020)

curricula in various classroom settings. In (i) learning outcomes, teachers may start with a needs analysis to diagnose students' aptitudes, learning needs and preferences to facilitate digital curriculum planning. Students need to be fully informed of course descriptions and learning outcomes, namely mastery of literacy skills in a virtual environment as listed in the reading-and-writing portfolio programme. More importantly, teachers should debrief students about assessment criteria and rubrics, so that students fully understood what they are expected to perform before the course/programme begins. In (ii) methodology, an effective e-Portfolio curriculum should include diverse types of instruction, e.g. audio-only (like a podcast), live video-conferencing meetings, pre-recorded lectures (via voiced-over presentation software) or a blended mode in which some students attend in-person classes and some online classes concomitantly. In any case, teachers should provide students with a succinct study schedule to indicate whether class meetings are conducted synchronously or asynchronously in order that they do not miss respective classes or hand in assignments late.

Similarly, in (iii) communication patterns, unlike face-to-face instruction, teachers need to make themselves available for clarifications, feedback, additional tutorials or online discussions at various junctures of e-Portfolio instruction. In some contexts, although e-Portfolios are implemented alongside in-person teaching in curricula, teachers or technical support staff members need to let students know when and how they can be approached if students encounter difficulties in compiling and managing artefacts. Creating an educational community within e-Portfolio programmes is practical, since teachers can utilise this community to initiate training workshops and discussion groups to promote student–student and student–teacher interactions. Lastly, in (iv), teachers should let students know the timeframe and frequency of formative and summative assessment tasks in e-Portfolio curricula beforehand. For instance, students should know how many written genres they need to compile for summative evaluation and what other multimedia artefacts will be counted towards their final grades. If reflective pieces are only assessed formatively, when and how students should hand them in (i.e. confidentiality issues) and what types of feedback they can obtain from the teacher should be considered. The assessment weightings/methods of online class participation or discussion groups should be explicitly explained to students, so that they can plan ahead their contribution in a systematic way.

Summary

Chapter 4 provided a roadmap for planning and implementing e-Portfolio curricula in L1 and L2 contexts. It first described the features and elements of e-Portfolio curricula, which characterised inquiry based, reflective and collaborative modes of instruction and entailed three unique elements: reflective learning, integrative pedagogy and authentic assessment. The chapter then illustrated how the teaching of four language skills was delivered in e-Portfolio curricula with authentic classroom examples. Furthermore, three approaches to facilitating e-Portfolio integration into English curricula were discussed amid three popular e-Portfolio programmes: the blended, provisional and personal approaches. Finally, Chapter 4 introduced a four-step curriculum convergence model to teachers who aspire to design and implement e-Portfolio programmes in their workplace.

5 E-Portfolios for Language Assessment

Introduction

Chapter 5 describes how to utilise e-Portfolios as an assessment method in language classrooms. It first introduces two fundamental assessment types with their accompanying paradigms, followed by a discussion on three dominant assessment purposes. Second, the chapter reviews the pros and cons of e-Portfolio assessment within a second language (L2) instructional context. Third, it discusses how and the extent to which e-Portfolios fulfil formative and summative assessment purposes differently with practical classroom-based strategies. In conclusion, Chapter 5 reveals how teachers can align language teaching, learning and assessment via e-Portfolios.

Assessment Types and Purposes

In language assessment, there are two broad assessment types: conventional and alternative assessments. Conventional assessment refers to paper-and-pencil tests, which evaluate learners' literacy skills in relation to external competency standards. It is formal, timed, impromptu and standardised (Green, 2020). Common examples include multiple-choice questions, essay tests, true or false items or selected response assessments. Alternative assessment takes place inside and outside the classroom, requiring students to display their linguistic competency by performing day-to-day authentic tasks, such as role-playing a dialogue or an act in a play, group writing assignments and note-taking listening tasks. It evaluates learners' high-order thinking and study skills, namely creativity, problem-solving, analytical and communication skills (Green, 2020). Alternative assessment is informal, authentic, collaborative and open-ended. Popular examples include oral presentation tasks, independent projects, portfolio work and self and peer assessments. These two assessment types originate from two paradigms, with conventional assessment under a positivist paradigm and alternative assessment under a constructivist paradigm. The positivist assessment paradigm emphasises fairness, standardisation and scoring reliability, whereas the constructivist assessment paradigm underscores meaning-making, diversity and content validity (Crusan & Ruecker, 2022).

In many parts of the world, conventional assessment remains predominant since it is relatively easy to grade and administer compared to alternative assessment. Additionally, conventional assessment has high scoring reliability and practicality (i.e. lower costs to administer a test with a large population of test-takers), although it may create negative washback effects, including test anxiety and narrowing of curricula (Black & Wiliam, 2018). Conventional assessment has moderate to low authenticity, given that it tends to adopt discrete-point items, which are both contrived and less relatable to test-takers' daily lives. In contrast, alternative assessment has been high on curriculum reform agendas in some regions, where the assessment *for* learning movement has become a regular classroom feature, such as in Britain, Sweden, Australia, New Zealand, Singapore and Hong Kong (Black, 2015; Klenowski, 2009). It has high content validity, authenticity and positive washback since language learning tasks can be adopted as assessment tasks interchangeably. Despite its authenticity and positive washback, alternative assessment could be costly to administer. For instance, one-on-one oral tests are exorbitant because exam boards need to pay for examiners' salaries, their training and venues, not to mention the monetary resources involved in conducting territory- and district-wide standardisation meetings.

Assessment has three purposes: formative, summative and ipsative. The formative purpose supports student learning. The summative purpose evaluates student learning, whereas the ipsative purpose facilitates students' self-assessment of language learning with reference to their previous work and external accountability standards (Lam, 2018a). Alternatively, the formative purpose of assessment equates to assessment *for* learning (effective pedagogy); the summative purpose assessment *of* learning (validated tests with success criteria); and the ipsative purpose assessment *as* learning (development of one's metacognition). This chapter discusses the first two assessment purposes, formative and summative assessments, because ipsative assessment is considered a sub-category of formative assessment as well. Formative assessment refers to effective feedback that assists students to close their learning gaps and supports self- and co-regulations of learning. It characterises academic growth, learning trajectories and the utilisation of feedback to fine-tune instruction (Magno & Lizada, 2015). The attributes of formative assessment tasks are continuous, bite-sized, student centred, feedback-rich and low-stakes (Gu, 2021). Summative assessment alludes to the formal evaluation of students' language proficiency near the end of an instructional unit or a semester. It emphasises internal and external reporting functions and determines whether students can progress to the next level of learning (Dixson & Worrell, 2016). The attributes of summative assessment tasks are short-lived, one-off, teacher centred, standardised in test conditions and high-stakes (Gu, 2021).

In educational assessment, scholars have observed the detrimental tensions between formative and summative assessments. They have noticed that summative assessment tends to take centre stage, while formative assessment is mostly marginalised, especially in exam-driven learning contexts (Guo & Yan, 2019). Some scholars depict summative assessment as negative and de-motivational, whereas formative assessment is seen as positive and beneficial to learning enhancement (Nevisi & Hosseinpur, 2022). Some liken summative assessment to a real thing, yet see formative assessment as a luxury. Despite these somewhat harmful dichotomies, researchers have understood that summative assessment may not necessarily be undesirable to language instruction, while formative assessment can only be beneficial to student learning when teachers and students possess a certain level of language assessment literacy (Dixson & Worrell, 2016). Instead, theorists have argued that formative and summative assessments serve different educational purposes. Hence, we cannot presume that one is better than the other, particularly when the two assessment methods can complement each other in a productive manner (Lam, 2013; Lau, 2016). For a long time, Harlen (2005: 220) suggested that 'the synergy of formative and summative assessment comes from making use of the same evidence for the two purposes'. For instance, teachers may use summative assessment formatively (i.e. using assessment results to adjust instruction, such as the re-teaching of some problematic grammatical structures) or adopt formative assessment summatively (i.e. effort grades to encourage revision of drafts and peer response activities). The next section discusses the advantages and limitations of e-Portfolio assessment.

Advantages and Drawbacks of e-Portfolio Assessment

Using e-Portfolios as an assessment method has become a trend, especially during and after the COVID-19 pandemic. In the past few years, home-based learning and remote instruction have become a new normal, as has e-assessment. Shifting language assessment online appears to be inevitable, since this option is economically, educationally and technologically viable and flexible, not to mention its compatibility with the modern-day language assessment landscape (Cooper *et al.*, 2022). The benefits of e-Portfolio assessment in L2 classroom contexts are fourfold. First, L2 learners tend to make more grammatical errors than their first language (L1) counterparts when required to do essay tests under timed conditions. If learners are assessed by e-Portfolios, they have a longer timeframe to engage in digital multimodal composing (Li, 2021). Because of this, e-Portfolio is a fair assessment method for L2 test-takers compared to conventional assessment. Second, owing to its malleable and multimedia format, e-Portfolio assessment could effectively evaluate students' high-order thinking skills, such as creativity, problem-solving and analytical skills. Thus, it measures and showcases students' language abilities more precisely (i.e. an aspect of test reliability; Eynon & Gambino, 2017). Third, e-Portfolio assessment is in context and authentic, which simulates daily work tasks. It is likely to enhance test usefulness when e-Portfolio tasks can promote knowledge transfer and enhance students' readiness to enter job markets (Abrar-ul-Hassan *et al.*, 2021). Fourth, e-Portfolio assessment, one common form of e-assessment, is in sync with 21st-century curriculum reforms, including assessment *for/as* learning to upgrade language instruction; authentic assessment to promote teachers' continuous professional development; and the dynamic use of feedback information to enhance teacher and student feedback literacy (Carless & Boud, 2018; Lam, 2021b).

Regardless of the above advantages, e-Portfolio assessment has the following limitations. Initially, teachers may find it cognitively challenging to score multi-genre and multimodal e-Portfolio artefacts even with a tried-and-tested rubric. This is because an average e-Portfolio consists of audio, video, textual and graphic artefacts. Scoring them impartially requires a high level of professional knowledge. Teachers may then find it complex to grade reflective pieces in students' e-Portfolios (Bowman *et al.*, 2016). After all, the reflective genre is considered personalised and confidential, and is not supposed to be graded or shared in the public eye. Handling students' sensitive data such as their reflective entries could be a cause for concern (Yancey *et al.*, 2013). Additionally, teachers may encounter difficulties in authenticating student authorship because some portfolio tasks involve collaboration and are completed off-campus. Teachers can neither detect the originality of students' artefacts (even using plagiarism checking software) nor identify how much external assistance students have sought throughout the compilation process owing to the process-orientated nature of most e-Portfolio tasks (Yancey, 2019). Ultimately, when e-Portfolios are utilised for summative assessment, teachers may be unable to make an accurate evaluation of students' language proficiency or computer literacy skills, particularly if an e-Portfolio has a flashy and decorative look that may distract teachers' professional judgement (Butler, 2006).

Other pressing issues that restrict the applications of e-Portfolio assessment include the digital divide, (lack of) e-assessment training and infringement of privacy. The digital divide refers to a discrepancy between those who can and those who cannot access digital tools (Hockly & Dudeney, 2018). Students who are from economically disadvantaged families may not be able to afford electronic devices or pay for mobile internet plans to complete e-Portfolio assessment tasks off-campus. Even if the issue of technological infrastructure is resolved, students are required to receive systematic training in manipulating the various consoles and interfaces of designated e-Portfolio platforms. Likewise, teachers need to upgrade their e-assessment knowledge and skills via professional development workshops, given that new functions of e-Portfolio software keep emerging (Cho, 2018). Although e-Portfolio assessment is a viable and timely option other than in-person testing, it is likely to infringe students' privacy, such as public disclosure of academic performance, family issues, interpersonal relationships in school among many others if teachers and school leaders do not follow proper protocols (Wilson *et al.*, 2018). The subsequent section unpacks how e-Portfolios can be utilised to serve both formative and summative assessment purposes with actionable strategies and classroom examples.

E-Portfolios for Formative and Summative Assessment Purposes

Utilising e-Portfolios as an instructional method is commonplace, but adopting them to achieve both the formative and summative purposes of assessment requires an additional knowledge base and practical skills. If teachers plan to use e-Portfolio assessment to achieve its formative purpose, they may focus on three aspects: process of learning, developmental trajectories and metacognition (Lam, 2019). Process of learning refers to multiple opportunities for students to improve their language proficiency over time by way of task-based e-Portfolio assessment. Developmental trajectories encourage students to record their language learning longitudinally in order to close achievement gaps. Metacognition promotes reflective thinking and composing skills in e-Portfolio assessment. These three learning-orientated assessment elements empower students to be active knowledge constructors in the e-Portfolio compilation process and acquisitive learners who regularly monitor and review their learning progress with e-feedback.

In formative assessment, learning is supposed to take place in stages and emphasise how students master various language skills with respect to their set goals and external benchmarks (Clark, 2012). In language education, an evaluation of learning outcomes is a must but not necessarily a priority. Meanwhile, students are encouraged to keep track of their learning trajectories by performing self-assessment, peer assessment and self-reflection to develop a deeper awareness of how their language development is evolving. To fulfil the formative purpose of assessment via e-Portfolios, feedback is a crucial catalyst to promote self-regulation and co-regulation of learning, especially when the elements of e-Portfolio assessment (i.e. creation, curation, reflection and dissemination) dovetail properly with major self-regulatory learning procedures, including goal setting, monitoring, reviewing and adjusting both individually and collaboratively (Lam, 2022a). The following describes four actionable strategies concerning how to achieve the formative purpose of e-Portfolio assessment.

(1) Self-assessment appears to be a regular feature in e-Portfolio assessment, yet not all students, especially young learners, may know how, what and the extent to which they should evaluate their learning. To this end, teachers may provide students with an induction on what and how to self-assess their language profiles. For instance, teachers can ask students to identify *one* strength and *two* weaknesses among one of their e-Portfolio artefacts, namely their argumentative genre recently uploaded for submission (Pourdana & Tavassoli, 2022). When students perform this self-assessment task online, teachers can guide them to refer to specific statements/explanations listed in a scoring rubric. These metalinguistic statements could help students self-assess their writing performances more readily. To further facilitate this self-assessment task, teachers may consider uploading three annotated, rubric-referenced exemplars with high, medium and low performances in the form of PDF files (by hiding the authors' names and ID numbers), so that students can compare their self-assessments with those multi-level exemplars to understand what they have and have not achieved and what else they should improve by self-reflection or consultation with the teacher for advice (Zhu & To, 2022). While these teacher-scaffolded self-assessment activities may not necessarily promote learner autonomy, they at least draw students' attention concerning how to self-assess one's work with rubrics and exemplars.

(2) Scoring students' interim drafts and multimedia artefacts without grades, aka comment-only marking, is another option to achieve the formative purpose of e-Portfolio assessment. Comment-only marking is not new, and it helps students focus on their learning rather than their performance (Burns & Frangiosa, 2021). When students submit their drafts and artefacts online, teachers consider giving initial comments in the form of (written or audio) qualitative commentaries or descriptive feedback and invite students to make revisions, if necessary, on a designated e-Portfolio tool. Then, students respond to teacher feedback and revise their work in progress accordingly. In case students do not understand particular teacher feedback, they may demand explanations or clarifications through the live chat or chatroom of the e-Portfolio tool. Formal summative grading is suspended until students can make satisfactory revisions with rationale based upon teacher and self-feedback, whichever is deemed applicable (Kuepper-Tetzel & Gardner, 2021). Comment-only marking is pedagogically feasible for e-Portfolio assessment as it underscores process-oriented instruction and highlights the learning process instead of the learning products. Additionally, deferred evaluation has long been a feature of paper-based portfolio assessment (Lam, 2017b). If students want to know their grades at mid-term, they are encouraged to estimate their performance and compare it with the

final grade to be assigned by the teacher to evaluate whether their self-evaluation is dependable and why.

(3) Student-generated feedback, be it peer or self-feedback, is encouraged throughout e-Portfolio construction journeys, yet whether its quality is beneficial to enhancing language learning remains questionable. To harness the formative potential of e-Portfolio assessment, teachers could provide timely and professional advice on the quality of peer and self-feedback derived from peer response and self-reflection activities in e-Portfolio assessment (Guskey, 2022). By adopting a web-based word processing software such as Google Docs, teachers can get involved in peer response tasks as onlookers as well as commentators who participate by providing linguistic clues and corrective written feedback whenever students encounter difficulties in generating correct and contextualised peer feedback to their classmates (Saeed & Al Qunayeer, 2022). Additionally, teachers may respond to individual students' self-reflective pieces as 'checkpoints' in their forum posts, wiki pages, weblog entries, social media posts or PDF files. If teachers check on students' self-reflection regularly and formatively, students are likely to understand whether their set goals have been met; feel motivated to engage in language learning with teacher feedback; and develop a positive attitude towards e-Portfolios by an ever-increasing social presence in an online assessment environment (Lam, 2018b). To protect student privacy, prior consent must be sought from students (especially those under 18) and their parents to guarantee that self-reflection contents are kept confidential.

(4) In paper-based portfolio assessment, reflection is restricted to text-based documents. In e-Portfolio assessment, digital reflection becomes a new genre for students. For those who are struggling with writing, digital reflection provides an alternative route to review their learning in a multimodal format (Yancey, 2009). Since most reflective pieces are not summatively graded, students are encouraged to audio-record or video-record their inner voices as part of digital reflection artefacts on any mobile device (Cheng & Chau, 2009). In addition, by using wireless stylus pens, students can draw pictures, take notes or create electronic presentation slides to capture their unique language development episodes as self-reflective pieces. For more advanced students with a higher level of digital competence, they may produce a vlog or create a video-hosting channel (restricted access to participants such as the teacher, the principal, friends or parents) to reveal the ups and downs of their language learning journeys in the format of a memoir or a narrative. By so doing, students can practice their electronic technology skills (video making/editing), communication skills (audience awareness building), creativity (storyboard creation) and

composing skills (script writing) when performing digital reflection (Silver, 2016). Not only do these e-Portfolio formative processes enhance students' L2 learning and computer literacy skills, but they also prioritise digital reflection as an instance of learning-orientated assessment (Clark, 2016).

Regardless of the formative potentials of e-Portfolio assessment, teachers eventually need to evaluate students' L2 learning for grading purposes, as summative assessment is essential in compulsory and higher education. Students cannot evade summative assessment. Hence, adopting e-Portfolio assessment to fulfil its summative purpose needs to be sensitive and strategic because grades may have negative impacts on students' learning (Guskey & Brookhart, 2019). If teachers plan to evaluate students' learning via e-Portfolios, they may consider the following three aspects: achievements, products of learning and e-Portfolio scores/grades (Lam, 2019). Achievements refer to evidence of learning that enables students to reach a milestone in their L2 development, e.g. a video clip showcasing a prize-winning moment in an inter-school duologue competition. Products of learning is about a formal evaluation of tangible learning artefacts, such as final drafts, an edited podcast or a revised project proposal compiled in an e-Portfolio platform. E-Portfolio scores or grades, assigned by the teacher against a comprehensive scoring guide, can indicate students' actual linguistic and digital competence, both in classroom-based assessments and large-scale testing.

Since the grading purpose of e-Portfolio assessment tends to be high-stakes, teachers should judge the quality of e-Portfolios using multiple methods to arrive at an impartial judgement while providing instructional benefits. For instance, teachers may evaluate students' e-Portfolios with a letter *grade* (A+, A, B, to C− or D) by impression marking; a numerical *score* (90%, 85%–45% the passing score) based on an artefact–coherence–presentation–language holistic rubric; *pass or fail* as one course/programme requirement; grades or scores linked to respective *success criteria, analytical rubrics* (with a detailed breakdown of each domain criteria) and *exemplars*; an average of student self-evaluation and teacher evaluation scores on mutual agreement (an instance of standardisation); an aggregation of student self-evaluation, peer evaluation and teacher evaluation scores with different weightings (i.e. 25%, 15% and 60%, respectively); and an overall grade followed by a student-and-teacher conference to discuss the student's strengths and weaknesses. With the above assessment methods, students can have a better idea of where they are now, how they got there and where they can go next, especially when multimedia feedback and revision opportunities are made possible in e-Portfolios. The following illustrates three pragmatic strategies that support the attainment of summative e-Portfolio assessment.

(1)   One method of scoring students' e-Portfolios summatively is to focus on their achievements. Teachers need to set explicit criteria of what artefacts or evidence of learning are considered students' representative work for showcasing their achievements and share with them in class. For instance, teachers can invite students to (a) choose the best genre they have ever composed that demonstrates their digital multimodal composing skills, be it a PDF, a podcast, a vlog among others; (b) choose an audio or a vlog with the most view counts in the past three months; and (c) choose trophies, awards or certificates won in any inter-school competitions. In addition to selecting representative work, students are required to compose a brief justification concerning why they selected those artefacts to represent their achievements and sign an agreement that these selections are final for summative evaluation (Cicchino *et al.*, 2019). In this method, teachers only evaluate students' most outstanding work instead of their reflective pieces, justifications and unfinished/unedited artefacts. To avoid dishonesty, teachers may check on students' other non-submitted work to ensure that they do not pretend to simply create and submit a few 'best' pieces without experiencing the entire compilation, curation, selection and reflection processes in e-Portfolios.

(2)   While teachers tend to grade students' e-Portfolios for the mid-term or the exam, they may also encourage students to link the making of this final product (a complete e-Portfolio) to reflections and other evidence of learning archived in an e-Portfolio platform. In this way, students are allowed to narrate their L2 learning experiences and justify what they learned when they curated those multimodal artefacts. To reduce the stakes of summative e-Portfolio assessment, teachers can break down a 100% score to a tripartite assessment weighting, namely a product grade (60%), a process grade (20%) and a participation grade (20%; Lam, 2020). The product grade is based on an evaluation of the student's complete e-Portfolio, whereas the process grade is based on an overview of the student's learning trajectory, including consultations with the teacher, self-directed learning episodes and any work in progress. The participation grade relies on teacher observation and learning management system (LMS) log data gathered from all LMS activities, such as forum contributions, login duration and frequency of downloads for flipped instructional materials. By using this tripartite assessment weighting, teachers can make a fairer and more holistic judgement on students' e-Portfolio learning, since e-Portfolio assessment is supposed to be process orientated, collaborative and participatory.

(3)   Assigning students a grade against a well-constructed rubric can demystify assessment requirements and enable students to understand how they are evaluated. There are two common rubrics in language

assessment: a holistic and an analytical scoring rubric (Crusan & Ruecker, 2022). The former comprehensively assesses a student's e-Portfolio by various levels of performance, such as exemplary, proficient, basic and sub-standard accompanied by respective descriptions (see Table 5.1). The latter appraises a student's e-Portfolio more specifically by utilising several domains, namely e-Portfolio content (inclusiveness of multimodal artefacts), design (aesthetics of interface), depth of reflection (degree of reflective practices), portfolio management skills (compilation and curation), etc., along with corresponding explanations plus levels of performance (see Table 5.2). By using rubrics in summative e-Portfolio assessment, teachers can save time on marking and find it easier to communicate assessment criteria with students. They can also enhance the reliability of e-Portfolio scoring if they apply the same rubric consistently. On the other hand, constructing a rubric requires a sophisticated level of assessment literacy and thus could be time-consuming. Following a rubric too closely is likely to make e-Portfolio scoring too restrictive as each e-Portfolio is unique, creative and complex in content (Lam, 2019).

Table 5.1 Holistic scoring rubric

Performance	Description	Commentary
Exemplary (Grade A/100%–85%)	The e-Portfolio contains a broad range of multimedia artefacts that document and showcase one's language learning. It is well organised and easily accessed by its audience. Its content is regularly updated and upgraded. Rich evidence is used to link with online reflection and self-assessment tasks to enhance learning.	
Proficient (Grade B/84.9%–70%)	The e-Portfolio contains different multimedia artefacts that properly document and showcase one's language learning. It is organised and can be accessed by its audience. Its content is updated occasionally. Adequate evidence is used to link with online reflection and self-assessment tasks to enhance learning.	
Basic (Grade C/69.9%–55%)	The e-Portfolio contains limited multimedia artefacts that partially document one's language learning. Its artefacts are randomly archived and may not be easily accessed by its audience. Its content is rarely updated. Insufficient but clear evidence is used to link with online reflection and self-assessment tasks to enhance learning.	
Sub-standard (Grade D or below/54.9%–30%)	The e-Portfolio contains few multimedia artefacts that do not constitute a 'proper' digital dossier. Its audience may probably find it hard to read or follow its content owing to its perfunctory nature. No trace of learning evidence is identified in relation to any online reflection or self-assessment tasks to enhance learning.	

Table 5.2 Analytical scoring rubric

Performance index/domain	Excellent	Very good	Good	Unsatisfactory	Score
E-Portfolio content and language proficiency (creation) 40%	Remarkably adept at creating a wide range of multimodal artefacts with a good command of language proficiency (40–36)	Skilful in creating various multimodal artefacts with high language proficiency (35–30)	Able to create multimodal artefacts with acceptable language proficiency (29–22)	Marginally include a few random artefacts with sub-standard language proficiency (21 or below)	=/40%
E-Portfolio management skills (curation) 20%	Highly proficient in organising and managing e-Portfolio content to support language learning (20–18)	Competent in organising and managing e-Portfolio content to improve language learning (17–15)	Showing fundamental management skills to organise and curate e-Portfolio content (14–12)	E-Portfolio content and artefacts are haphazardly and incoherently displayed (11–6)	=/20%
Depth of reflection (reflection) 20%	Engaging in a very deep and critical level of reflection to showcase language learning (20–18)	Engaging in a deep level of reflection to showcase language learning (17–15)	Engaging in a moderate level of reflection to showcase language learning (14–12)	Engaging in a low level of reflection which hardly showcases language learning (11–6)	=/20%
E-Portfolio format and design (dissemination) 20%	Interface facilitates viewing, browsing and online sharing (20–18)	Interface is considered viewer-friendly and accessible (17–15)	Interface is marginally viewer-friendly and not accessible due to some design faults (14–12)	Interface is hard to view, browse and communicate with audience (11–6)	=/20%
Total score:					=/100%

The ensuing section unpacks how teachers synergise L2 teaching, learning and assessment through e-Portfolios.

Aligning Teaching, Learning and Assessment via e-Portfolios

In conventional English curricula, the teaching–learning–assessment process is linear and undynamic. Assessment takes place after instruction has finished and its major format is paper-and-pencil tests. It is typically used as a high-impact summative tool to measure student learning and teacher instruction near the end of a school year. In other words, the formative and summative purposes of L2 assessment remain mutually exclusive and pedagogically separated. In e-Portfolio assessment, with careful planning and design, teachers are more likely to integrate assessment into L2 instruction. For instance, self-reflection and self and peer assessment tasks are, by default, regular features in the e-Portfolio compilation process. Requiring students to assess their own learning and their peers' learning has become an integral part of learning in an e-Portfolio environment (Dann, 2017; Lam *et al.*, 2023). The constructive alignment of assessment and L2 learning is considered natural and legitimate in alternative assessment, such as e-Portfolio assessment, particularly when in-person instruction was interrupted during and after the pandemic.

In e-Portfolio assessment, the teaching–learning–assessment sequence could be flexibly shuffled by positioning 'assessment' before teaching and learning as a diagnostic formative assessment task. 'Bite-sized formative assessments' may also happen at the intervals of the assessment–teaching–learning–assessment sequence to gradually scaffold student learning (see Figure 5.1). The integration of assessment into L2 instruction facilitates self-regulation in learning, since bite-sized formative assessments enable students to seamlessly curate, monitor and review their L2 learning via their e-Portfolio artefacts. Similarly, the implementation of strategy-based writing instruction in e-Portfolio programmes can synergise L2 instruction and assessment constructively because teaching of and assessing with self-regulatory skills take place simultaneously (Teng, 2022). The above

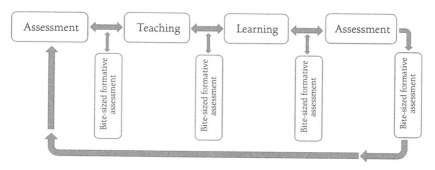

Figure 5.1 Teaching–learning–assessment sequence in e-Portfolio assessment

positive alignment of L2 teaching, learning and assessment has several advantages. First, the alignment upgrades pedagogy and student learning (Black & Wiliam, 2018). Second, it lowers the stakes of summative e-Portfolio assessment. Third, it increases student motivation, as learning tasks are, in fact, assessment tasks that familiarise students with the test format (Lam, 2013). Fourth, the practice of aligning instruction and assessment empowers teachers' language assessment literacy (Gan & Lam, 2022). Fifth, integrating L2 learning and assessment undoubtedly enhances learner autonomy and language awareness.

Summary

Chapter 5 described the use of e-Portfolios as an assessment method in L2 settings. It first introduced what conventional and alternative assessments are and how they differ conceptually. The chapter then unpacked the rationale behind the formative and summative purposes of e-Portfolio assessment and their dichotomous debates in language assessment research. It subsequently explained the advantages and limitations of e-Portfolio assessment when applied at the classroom level. Next, it illustrated how e-Portfolios could fulfil formative and summative assessment purposes with justifications and practical classroom strategies. Finally, the chapter provided readers with suggestions on how to align teaching, learning and assessment via e-Portfolios to facilitate effective L2 education.

6 Case Study 1: Students' Perceptions of e-Portfolio Assessment Literacy

Introduction

Chapter 6 reports on a pilot study, examining a group of 34 adolescent students' perceptions on the use of e-Portfolios as a second language (L2) learning tool. The pilot study was part of a larger study that investigated secondary-level students' perceived e-Portfolio assessment literacy when home-based learning was introduced. First, Chapter 6 unpacks three components of learners' e-Portfolio assessment literacy and how they might facilitate L2 learning. Second, it describes the study by detailing its informants, context, instruments and data analysis. Third, key findings are presented in accordance with the three components of e-Portfolio assessment literacy. The chapter ends with a discussion of pedagogical implications.

E-Portfolio Assessment Literacy

To conceptualise this pilot study, the idea of e-Portfolio assessment literacy is expounded. E-Portfolio assessment literacy comprises three major components: compilation, conceptions of assessment and emotional experience. E-Portfolio compilation refers to how adolescents create, curate, revise and disseminate digital artefacts, whereas conceptions allude to their perceptions of e-Portfolio assessment. Emotional experience is about adolescents' affective response when they embark on e-Portfolio journeys (Crisol Moya *et al.*, 2021).

Regarding compilation, students tend to find e-Portfolio development more gratifying and enlightening than paper-based portfolios, given that the former is somewhat accessible, convenient and easy for retrieval. Students are particularly keen on creating multimedia artefacts by self-selecting their preferred topics, registers, modalities and presentation software (Madden *et al.*, 2019). In both mediums of portfolios, students equally put a premium on enacting active agency and autonomy in the L2 learning process (Sharifi *et al.*, 2017). While e-Portfolio assessment is said to be learner centred and contextualised, some e-Portfolio programmes remain highly prescriptive and require students to comply with stringent submission guidelines. These programmes render participants limited (meta-)cognitive capacity for creating, curating, reflecting and showcasing their best works over time, not to mention those restrictive instructions which run counter to the principles of e-Portfolio assessment – socio-constructivism (Farrell, 2020; Lam, 2018a, 2022a). While most studies investigated the short- to middle-term effects of e-Portfolio compilation on student learning and yielded favourable results, little has been done to understand its long-term impact. Contrary to popular belief, students prefer continuing to maintain and upgrade their e-Portfolios even beyond graduation, although they may lack the appropriate computer and language learning skills to curate and reflect on digital artefacts in the longer term (Clarke & Boud, 2018).

Regarding conceptions of e-Portfolio assessment, students usually hold affirmative attitudes towards the method, especially when e-Portfolio assessment is considered a better alternative to conventional impromptu essay testing (Baturay & Daloğlu, 2010). Used as an innovative L2 learning approach, students have a balanced view of its learning and grading functions of assessment. Based upon some studies, students believed that they could set, monitor and review their learning goals with reference to their language competence as required by designated L2 programmes (Chang *et al.*, 2018). They also felt that e-Portfolio assessment could enhance their language skills, such as reading, writing, speaking and vocabulary (Yancey, 2019; Zheng & Barrot, 2022). Additionally, students noticed that they had marked improvement in peer assessment skills, for instance, providing accurate peer feedback despite the fact that a majority of them remained sceptical about the learning potential of peer feedback when compared to teacher feedback (Nicol *et al.*, 2019). For summative assessment, students felt that e-Portfolios could serve their purpose by helping them achieve satisfactory to good final grades in a course. Although students usually considered e-Portfolio assessment fulfilling, practical and rewarding when they curated and reflected upon their learning via multimedia artefacts on an e-Portfolio platform, some of them still thought that e-Portfolio keeping was tedious, cumbersome and time-consuming, and that they needed to put in a lot of effort to compile and upgrade their e-Portfolio contents regularly (Aydin, 2014).

Considering learners' emotional experience, research shows that if students develop positive emotions towards their L2 learning, they tend to perform better in their academic results as well as enhancing their self-efficacy and levels of confidence (Kusuma & Waluyo, 2023). Within the context of e-Portfolio assessment, positive emotion experience includes active participation in a community of practice (speedy sharing and wide dissemination via e-Portfolio platforms), trust in teachers' summative judgements of their artefacts and multiple opportunities to revise and reflect on L2 learning (Deneen *et al.*, 2018). In contrast, students' negative emotion is mostly concerned with infringement of privacy since e-Portfolio contents could easily be leaked even with password-protected functions. Students also feel strongly about the issue of fairness in e-Portfolio assessment, because scoring an e-Portfolio is probably a subjective undertaking (Yancey, 2015). Studies on the nexus of emotion and L2 learning further indicated that if students enjoyed engaging in the e-Portfolio process and felt assured with the overall experience, they were likely to make more 'investments' in learning owing to a heightened sense of ownership, achievement and belonging (Pourdana & Tavassoli, 2022). In other words, emotion plays a crucial role in affecting the uptake of e-Portfolio knowledge and skills when students are acquiring an L2. Taken together, this study aimed to examine adolescent learners' perceptions of e-Portfolio assessment literacy in two Hong Kong secondary schools. The next section presents how this study was conducted.

The Study

Informants

The pilot study took place in two Hong Kong top-tier secondary-level schools where the medium of instruction was English. Students studying in high-performing schools represented the top 15%–25% of the entire student population across the territory. Thirty-four students (26 male and eight female students) agreed to complete an online questionnaire and nine of them further agreed to be interviewed by their English teachers. These 34 respondents were considered more capable students approximately equivalent to learners of lower C1 to upper B2 levels of the Common European Framework of Reference for Languages. In an online questionnaire, a majority of the respondents (94.1%) used digital gadgets daily and had prior experience of using e-Portfolios. Of the respondents, 100% said that they were confident in using instant messaging apps (e.g. WhatsApp) and 70.6% said that they sometimes used academic apps such as online dictionaries and Grammarly. The respondents also applied three common computer skills: information search (94.1%), word processing (79.4%) and presentation software (50%). Generally, most respondents were computer literate although they were not necessarily able to manoeuvre e-Portfolio functions proficiently.

Context

The pilot study was conducted between January and mid-April 2022 when the fifth wave of the pandemic hit Hong Kong. Because of the soaring daily confirmed COVID-19 cases, the Education Bureau called for class suspension among K-12 schools. During this period, distance learning and remote teaching (via video-conferencing apps like Zoom) replaced in-person instruction. Additionally, language assessment such as tests, quizzes and uniform tests adopted the online mode, except for the final examination which took place in school around late June or early July. Both English teachers in the two participating schools adopted Google Classroom as a default e-Portfolio platform and followed a school-based curriculum as assigned by respective heads of department. The student informants had a one-time experience of using e-Portfolios during the previous class suspension (i.e. mid-December 2020 to March 2021). As the informants had prior knowledge and experience of e-Portfolios, our research team wanted to explore their perceived e-Portfolio assessment literacy through three research instruments that will be described below.

Instruments

The study utilised an online questionnaire ($n = 34$), semi-structured interviews ($n = 9$) and e-Portfolio contents ($n = 6$) to investigate students' e-Portfolio assessment literacy. The questionnaire items were adapted from two tried-and-tested instruments in two published studies (Bolliger & Shepherd, 2010; Ritzhaupt et al., 2008). These two instruments were further reworded based upon qualitative feedback collected from two Hong Kong-based and one US-based language teaching scholars. With their feedback, our team piloted the second last revised version with another five secondary-level students not involved in this project. According to their response, we made one more round of minor revisions by modifying some ambiguous wording. The final questionnaire has six parts: demographic information, previous experience, e-Portfolio compilation, conceptual understanding, emotional experiences and open-ended questions (see Appendix A). Except for open-ended questions, all items used a 5-point Likert scale, from Strongly Agree to Strongly Disagree. Regarding the interview guide, we drafted nine questions and invited the co-investigator plus one overseas scholar to comment. Question 7 was slightly reworded due to lack of clarity and one question was deleted owing to an overlap (see Appendix B). Of the 34 respondents, we selected six students' e-Portfolios to perform content analysis. The six students' portfolio work represented a spectrum of academic abilities, namely two high, three middle and one low performance.

Analysis

Our team adopted qualitative data analysis. For the questionnaire data, our team utilised descriptive statistics to report the means and standard deviations of each item. As to the open-ended questions and student interview transcripts, we performed electronic plus manual coding three times (i.e. 2 + 1) and organised these codes thematically to reveal emerging themes. Regarding the students' e-Portfolios, we used qualitative content analysis to find out what e-Portfolio artefacts the informants had created and curated, and to triangulate with their perceptions of e-Portfolio assessment literacy.

Results

Online questionnaire

Parts 1 and 2 data were briefly reported in the section titled 'Informants'. In this section, we present data from Parts 3 to 6, which have 12, 16, 17 and 4 items, respectively. Part 3 was about students' perceptions of e-Portfolio compilation during distance learning. Of 12 items, students' perceptions remained mostly positive with an average mean score of 3.48 (highest mean of $M = 3.91$ in Item 1 and lowest mean of $M = 2.79$ in Item 7). The majority of the students agreed that e-Portfolio expectations were clearly stated in the course, which implied that there were effective student–teacher communications in a virtual learning environment ($M = 3.91$). More importantly, most students admitted that they would browse others' e-Portfolios in the future, which showed a sustainable learning attribute as students could only view their classmates' e-Portfolios in the same school ($M = 3.76$). Likewise, a large number of students considered teacher feedback on their e-Portfolios as constructive criticism, which showed a trusted attitude towards the accuracy and timeliness of teacher feedback ($M = 3.71$). Although students were eager to showcase their e-Portfolios with fellow classmates, they were not enthusiastic about sharing their work with families probably owing to privacy ($M = 2.79$). In Item 9, students felt that they could learn from their mistakes via e-Portfolio compilation, indicating the development of a reflective stance when creating and curating different digital artefacts ($M = 3.59$). As said, students' perceptions of e-Portfolio compilation remained encouraging although some students had reservations about sharing their work with families.

Part 4 was about students' conceptions of e-Portfolio assessment for L2 learning. The average mean score for this part was 3.59. The highest mean score was 3.85 in Items 3 and 10 and the lowest mean score was 3.15 in Item 12. Hence, students were mainly positive about both the summative and formative purposes of assessment. Of the 34 students, 26 agreed that using e-Portfolios could help teachers assess their knowledge summatively ($M = 3.85$). Similarly, 26 students believed that browsing classmates' e-Portfolios enhanced their understanding of and reflection on L2 learning formatively ($M = 3.85$). This item (Item 10) dovetailed with Items 14 and 15 ($M = 3.71$ and 3.68), respectively, in which student respondents believed that browsing their peers' e-Portfolios was a worthwhile plus beneficial learning experience. This finding implied that e-Portfolios were likely to facilitate formative peer assessment despite student scepticism about peer feedback. Another intriguing finding was identified in Item 4, in which 24 students considered that using e-Portfolios could help them reach their learning goals by upgrading their computer and language skills ($M = 3.82$). Overall, students' perceptions of e-Portfolio assessment were affirmative, given that students regarded e-Portfolios as a 'better' assessment method than conventional multiple-choice and essay testing (M = 3.65).

Part 5 was about students' emotional experience of e-Portfolio compilation. The respondents displayed more positive than negative emotion, with an average mean score of 3.67 in 17 items. The highest mean score was 4.26 in Item 15, whereas the lowest was 3.06 in Item 8. For positive emotion, in Item 3, 29 students found e-Portfolios easy to use with steady access to the internet (M = 4.09). In Item 13, 27 students stated that they felt comfortable with e-Portfolios graded by teachers in a course (M = 4.03). The results showed student satisfaction with the e-Portfolio experience in terms of daily operation and summative assessment. In Part 4 (Items 14 and 15), although two-thirds of the students thought highly of peer learning via e-Portfolios, only 14 of them liked sharing their e-Portfolios with their classmates in Item 8 (M = 3.06), which implied that students might not necessarily like sharing artefacts with schoolmates, especially those involving personal matters. This intriguing finding had repercussions for what respondents demanded in Item 15, where they hoped that the confidentiality of their e-Portfolio could be guaranteed (M = 4.26). In addition, many students hoped that their portfolio artefacts would turn into useful work (M = 4.21 in Item 16) and could be judged objectively (M = 4.18 in Item 17). These findings demonstrated that the respondents might not experience negative emotion, but they had concerns with certain aspects of the e-Portfolio process, namely protection of privacy and fair teacher summative judgement.

Part 6 was four open-ended questions, including an understanding of e-Portfolios, support for creating e-Portfolios, benefits and drawbacks of e-Portfolio keeping and likes and dislikes about e-Portfolios. Question 1 had 26 responses. Our team used coding followed by frequency count, and further summarised all responses. The findings showed that respondents perceived e-Portfolios as a digital dossier of student work (n = 7); a tool for information exchange (n = 6); a learning-assisted platform (n = 6); and a system for homework submission and collection (n = 6). Only one student deemed e-Portfolios as software to track student learning formatively. This finding implied that e-Portfolios were considered a learning management system for managing assignment storage, submission and collection during home-based learning. Question 2 had 28 responses, 7 of which reported that they got *no* support and 21 of which received support from various sources, namely teacher instruction (n = 10), extra study materials (n = 7) and related software tools (n = 4). This finding suggested that teacher scaffolding in e-Portfolio integration remained indispensable.

Twenty-seven valid responses were identified in Question 3. Of the 27 respondents, 23 (85.2%) described benefits and 8 (29.6%) reported drawbacks. For the benefits of e-Portfolios, most students said that they were convenient (n = 10), interactive (n = 4), efficient (n = 3) and easy to use ($n = 3$). For the drawbacks of e-Portfolios, the eight students believed that e-Portfolios were inconvenient when used asynchronously ($n = 5$), time-consuming ($n = 2$) and somewhat distracting by pop-up ads ($n = 1$). In Question 4, our team categorised 28 responses into positive and negative emotion experience. Of these, 25 were coded as positive responses and 3 as negative. Among the positive responses, students mainly felt that e-Portfolios were convenient, up to date (paperless), organised, safe and useful, whereas among the negative responses, one said that e-Portfolios lacked the human touch. The above findings corresponded to the published research that students' perceptions of e-Portfolio application remained encouraging although not without its challenges (cf. Song, 2021).

Semi-structured interview

Two student interview transcripts were coded three times. The codes were then categorised in accordance with the three components of e-Portfolio assessment literacy – compilation, conceptions of assessment and emotion experience. For compilation, interviewees said that it was relatively straightforward and convenient to construct e-Portfolios as their teachers had already set up the template on Google Classroom. To them, using Google Classroom as an e-Portfolio platform was highly organised and it was easy to retrieve their classwork and homework assignments anytime and anywhere. Selected interviewees also felt that using e-Portfolios was environmentally friendly, as they were paperless and only occupied cloud-based storage on the software. Despite these advantages, interviewees did encounter technological issues while assembling their e-Portfolios, namely unstable internet connection, uploading of artefacts with the right format and compatibility of the operating systems used in digital gadgets (e.g. iOS vs Android). In addition, interviewees realised that due to prescribed e-Portfolio templates, it was less likely to personalise their e-Portfolio compilation, such as layout, organisation and medium of artefacts.

Regarding conceptions of assessment, interviewees found that e-Portfolios could serve both formative and summative purposes of assessment properly. For instance, students commended the timeliness of e-feedback via e-Portfolios, since teachers could give them instant feedback. Some interviewees mentioned that they set goals, reviewed the goals and reflected on language learning while curating multimedia artefacts throughout the e-Portfolio process. They enjoyed being able to review past and present learning in order to work on their improvement plans. Since interviewees were asked to complete online assignments during home-based learning, they could search, select and cite pertinent online resources to enhance the overall quality of their portfolio entries. By so doing, interviewees became more self-directed and self-motivated than completing paper-based assignments. As to summative grading, interviewees thought that e-Portfolios were a form of continuous assessment, so that they could progressively improve their learning by adopting teacher and peer feedback. When asked whether e-Portfolios were a fair assessment tool, four interviewees had confidence that their teachers could make unbiased judgement on their portfolio artefacts.

Interviewees had mixed views on emotion experience. On the plus side, students enjoyed using e-Portfolios to improve their language proficiency although they encountered technological challenges. Three out of five interviewees in one focus group stated that they had developed a sense of ownership towards their e-Portfolios and felt proud of what they had created over time. Another two students felt that the automated writing evaluation tools in e-Portfolio platforms, e.g. the provision of autocorrect and editorial suggestions, enabled them to make fewer errors and produced more coherent texts for submission. Interviewees also felt supported when the teacher gave them instant feedback to improve their work. Regardless of these merits, some students thought negatively about e-Portfolio assessment, especially when most e-Portfolio layouts were pre-set by their teachers. One student stated that he did not have a sense of achievement, since his task simply uploaded documents to corresponding folders. Another student expressed concerns about his declining motivation, since e-Portfolio assessment neither promoted active curation of artefacts nor required students to deeply reflect upon their learning in the course. However, he reiterated that this negative emotion was personal and some of his classmates remained motivated to engage in e-Portfolio tasks.

Student e-Portfolio content

Six students' e-Portfolio contents were qualitatively analysed according to layout, organisation, content, ability and reflection. In terms of *layout*, students' e-Portfolios were somewhat standardised since both schools (A and B) adopted Google Classroom as default e-Portfolio platforms. Nevertheless, two students changed the original template to a more colourful one with an eye-catching wallpaper featuring their idols 'BLACKPINK'; the other four simply followed their teachers' templates by using either orange and blue as background colours for Schools A and B, respectively. As regards *organisation*, students' artefacts were arranged by language skills (e.g. listening, reading comprehension, writing) and task titles (e.g. F.3 First Term Test Scope, Reported Speech Exercise, One-sided Argumentative Essay – Consumption Voucher). As shared by students, these headings and folders were pre-set by their teachers. They had no say but uploaded related work to the respective dossiers. The flow of portfolio headings was highly organised, clear and easily retrieved.

In School A, e-Portfolio *contents* mainly covered process writing, including pre-writing, while-writing and post-writing phases with adequate teacher input and collaborative writing tasks. Additionally, the process writing content consisted of self and peer assessment tasks, error correction tasks and online sharing of exemplars. Students' writing tasks were marked in long hand and uploaded onto Google Classroom as PDFs for correction. In School B, e-Portfolio *contents* comprised classwork, homework, marked worksheets and final composition drafts with much less teacher scaffolding and collaborative tasks. Concerning *ability*, high- and middle-level students performed satisfactorily on various tasks and their handwriting was much more legible than their low-performing counterparts. Interestingly, all six students made numerous typos and spelling mistakes in their writing tasks regardless of their academic abilities. There was a clear lack of *reflection* in e-Portfolios, except for three students in School A, who were asked to complete an error/progress log for review. In School B, there was no evidence that the three students had reviewed any e-Portfolio artefacts to reflect upon the strengths and weaknesses of their language abilities. Taken together, students' e-Portfolio contents in this study remained largely prescriptive, top-down, teacher centred and unreflective.

Discussion and Implications

This penultimate section discusses emergent issues arising from the above data sets and implications are proposed accordingly.

E-Portfolio compilation

Students' perceptions of e-Portfolio compilation were encouraging in the areas of understanding of objectives, self-reflective learning and peer assessment. In practicality, our team observed that the informants were required to comply with the homework policy set by the respective schools and the content of e-Portfolio artefacts was rather standardised and restrictive in terms of genres, modality and register. While students felt positive about the metacognitive role of e-Portfolios, their artefacts were less likely to materialise this instructional aspect because students were not given opportunities to self-assess their works in progress. Regardless of students' affirmative response about their compilation journeys, they did encounter some technical issues, e.g. uploading with the correct file size and format and manoeuvring the e-Portfolio interface properly (Lam *et al.*, 2023). Hence, teachers and researchers should not take for granted that their students can utilise e-Portfolios to support L2 learning automatically without training. There are two implications for this sub-section. First, e-Portfolio curricula should be made more stylistically diverse and inclusive in topics if the ultimate goal is to advocate creativity, individuality and linguistic competence (Yancey, 2019).

After all, e-Portfolio artefacts are anticipated to be divergent rather than convergent. Second, although students born in a digital age may have attained a certain level of computer literacy, explicit training in manipulating common e-Portfolio functions remains necessary since students are usually proficient in using instant messaging apps and playing computer games (Vahedi *et al.*, 2021). These two implications, indicating a need for flexible portfolio curricula and the provision of student training in using e-Portfolio software applications, dovetail with those studies published in neighbouring countries, such as Indonesia, Vietnam and Singapore, which encountered similar challenges when students engaged in respective e-Portfolio programmes for the first time (e.g. Kusuma & Waluyo, 2023; Nguyen *et al.*, 2023; Song, 2021).

Conceptions of assessment

Students' conceptions of e-Portfolio assessment were largely constructive as the informants believed that e-Portfolio assessment could assist teachers to make sound judgement of their L2 learning. They unanimously considered that e-Portfolios were a 'better' alternative to paper-and-pencil tests. Some informants regarded e-Portfolios as one form of continuous assessment, which helped track student learning periodically and provided timely feedback to support learning. Despite this, the informants equally appreciated the usefulness of peer assessment since they could reflect upon their own portfolio performance by making references to others' performance. Although the informants had a balanced view of the summative and formative purposes of e-Portfolio assessment, our team noticed that the practice of self-reflection and self and peer assessments remained few and far between, especially in School B where students were not asked to review any artefacts at mid-term or near end of term. Therefore, teachers may consider redirecting students' attention to formative assessment practices and help develop students' formative assessment literacy (Fukuda *et al.*, 2022). With this, two implications are proposed. First, e-Portfolio assessment should emphasise its summative and formative functions concurrently. For instance, teachers may assign *effort* or *progress* grades to encourage students to regularly participate in their portfolio work (cf. Chapter 5). Second, students' e-Portfolio performance can be utilised as a reference for fine-tuning teachers' L2 instruction, namely re-teaching certain weak areas or revamping the curriculum to accommodate students' learning needs. These two emerging findings align with those of comparable international studies, wherein teachers need to refocus on the formative purpose of e-Portfolio assessment rather than its summative purpose (i.e. using reflection to help students close the learning gaps; Clarke & Boud, 2018) as well as to use feedback generated from e-Portfolios to inform L2 instruction pedagogically (Barrett, 2010).

Emotion experience

Students' positive emotion prevailed over their negative emotion when they engaged in e-Portfolio construction, since they believed that e-Portfolios were easy to use and provided instant feedback for learning. Some informants developed ownership although the e-Portfolio templates were predetermined by teachers. The informants also felt that the integration of e-Portfolios into the curriculum was timely and legitimate, given that distance learning was the only solution when in-person instruction was abruptly suspended. Notwithstanding this positive emotion, the informants did raise concerns about a few issues. Although they enjoyed peer learning, they remained cynical about sharing their artefacts with peers. Furthermore, they hoped that their e-Portfolio assignments could be turned into useful digital artefacts so that they could review them in the future. Considering these emotions, two implications emerge. First, teachers may consider adopting a safe and high security e-Portfolio platform to increase students' willingness to share, disseminate and respond to each other's work. To warrant transparency and communication, teachers may inform students of the purpose and benefits of e-Portfolio assessment at the outset in order to dispel misconceptions. Second, it is necessary for teachers to help students transfer their insecurity (i.e. negative emotion) into positive emotion by providing scaffolding, instructional guidelines and moral support in a timely manner (i.e. encouragement; Crisol Moya et al., 2021). Hence, students do not feel that e-Portfolio compilation is a risky undertaking. Recently, two studies conducted in Vietnam reported similar findings by identifying a positive shift in students' attitudes and emotion after they engaged in Canvas-based and Flipgrid-based e-Portfolio programmes that assisted them in improving their English proficiency, namely their writing and speaking skills, respectively (Hanh & Huong, 2021; Le et al., 2023).

Summary

Chapter 6 reported on a pilot study that investigated 34 adolescent learners' perceptions of e-Portfolio assessment literacy. The chapter initially revealed the three major elements of e-Portfolio assessment literacy. Second, it described the methodology of the study by explaining its informants, context, instruments and data analysis. Third, the chapter presented qualitative data from online questionnaires, semi-structured interviews and e-Portfolio artefacts with regard to the three-pronged framework of e-Portfolio assessment literacy, namely e-Portfolio compilation, conceptions of e-Portfolio assessment and emotion experience. Chapter 6 concluded with a discussion section together with its pedagogical implications.

7 Case Study 2: E-Portfolio Integration during Pandemic and Beyond

Introduction

Chapter 7 is a case study on how two English teachers integrated e-Portfolio tools during the pandemic. The case study was derived from a larger study that examined students' and teachers' perceptions of e-Portfolio applications in Hong Kong English classrooms. First, Chapter 7 introduces how teachers transitioned from face-to-face to online instruction and the extent to which educational technology was integrated during the pandemic. It then describes the case study, including its design, informants, research context and instruments when e-Portfolio practices were thoroughly investigated in remote instruction and assessment. Afterwards, two case scenarios are reported based upon technology integration, affordances and constraints. Post-pandemic lessons learnt from the case study are also discussed. The chapter concludes with pedagogical implications of recommending how e-Portfolio integration could be made sustainable in second language (L2) settings.

Background

In February 2020, the COVID-19 pandemic triggered an unprecedented public health crisis and affected almost all walks of life worldwide, including aviation, tourism, manufacturing, medicine and education. Of these fields, education has been particularly hard-hit, since in-person classes were suspended incessantly for prolonged periods in different parts of the world, especially at the beginning of the pandemic (February–April 2020) and a later resurgence of confirmed COVID cases due to different virus variants (December 2020 to March 2021 and December 2021 to April 2022). Because of this, educational technology appeared to be a viable option to substitute for face-to-face instruction in K-12 contexts on a gigantic scale, e.g. extensive use of video-conferencing software and learning management systems, namely e-Portfolios to continue language teaching and learning (Daniel, 2020).

In online instruction and assessment, teachers mostly find it demanding to shift from in-person to virtual pedagogy overnight with minimal or even no preparation. Although educational technology was adopted long before the pandemic, it was largely restricted to e-books, presentation slides and game-based apps to increase student engagement. Large-scale technological integration into L2 classrooms appears to be sporadic (De Nito *et al.*, 2022). Externally, teachers reported that there was an apparent lack of training in technical skills (e.g. how to maximise teacher–student interactions on video-conferencing tools) and infrastructure (e.g. provision of free laptops or sponsorship of wifi subscription fees; Eynon, 2021). School culture, curriculum design and immediate teaching environments are regarded as external barriers that may promote or inhibit technology integration (Sailer *et al.*, 2021). Internally, teacher beliefs and attitudes towards computer-mediated language teaching is likely to determine the extent to which teachers integrate technological approaches into their instruction during class suspension (Wang, 2021).

With technology integration, e-Portfolios are considered a prominent medium of online instruction, which has been widely researched in language education in general (Yancey, 2019) and L2 writing in particular (Barrot, 2021). E-Portfolios help students to take stock of their learning via active compilation, curation and review of digital artefacts as evidence of learning to facilitate language development (Segaran & Hasim, 2021). Although e-Portfolios are usually perceived to be a better alternative to conventional instruction and assessment, they have pros and cons. On the plus side, e-Portfolios enhance teacher technological pedagogical content knowledge, autonomy and repertoire of instructional skills (Aygün & Aydin, 2016). On the minus side, e-Portfolios may create extra workload for teachers, resistance to using technology (teachers with lower levels of computer literacy) and emotional impact on teacher self-efficacy (peer pressure or institutional sanction if not applying technology in teaching; Cooper *et al.*, 2022). Regardless of this scholarship about online instruction and e-Portfolios, there is a dearth of research exploring the extent to which L2 teachers integrated technology in remote teaching from insiders' perspectives, and what affordances and constraints they encountered during the pandemic (Ligado *et al.*, 2022). This case study intended to fill this gap. Its overarching objective was to examine how two beginning L2 teachers initiated and developed their e-Portfolio programmes in online instruction, and what affordances and constraints of e-Portfolio integration they experienced during distance learning. The following section provides details of the study.

The Study

Design

The study adopted a case study approach by reporting on classroom, self-reported and documentary data collected over the pandemic. The rationale behind such a design was to gather insiders' perspectives on how e-Portfolios were integrated and what affordances and constraints were met by teacher informants during a 1.5-year window (Tondeur *et al.*, 2017). Without drawing upon teachers' first-hand experiences, the study could not generate rich and in-depth qualitative data to address the objectives of this chapter in a dependable and trustworthy way. The design was also aimed at enriching teachers' and scholars' conceptual understanding of e-Portfolio integration and affordances/challenges within a larger L2 classroom environment.

Informants

Two informants, Teachers A and B, were locally trained English teachers with three year's teaching experience at the time of writing. Both obtained bachelor's double degrees in English and language education from one Hong Kong university. After graduation, Teacher A worked in a Chinese-as-the-medium-of-instruction secondary school, where English was taught as a language subject and students' abilities were generally below average. Teacher B worked in an English-as-the-medium-of-instruction secondary school, where all subjects were taught in English except for Chinese and Chinese history and students' abilities were mostly above average. Both informants volunteered to join the study through an open call. Before the study, the two teachers had no experience or formal training in online teaching although they occasionally adopted popular game-based learning apps (e.g. Kahoot!) in their instruction.

Context

In Hong Kong, e-learning has been promoted for more than two decades. In schools, face-to-face teaching remains the norm and e-learning is restricted to the use of e-books, PowerPoint software and some digital games. Large-scale remote teaching is uncommon. From mid-November 2019, Hong Kong schools underwent five rounds of class suspensions because of the social movement (i.e. large-scale university student protests) and five waves of the COVID-19 pandemic. During class suspensions, online teaching and learning became a new normal. The initial class suspension happened in mid-November 2019 and lasted for a week. The second class suspension occurred between early February 2020 and late May 2020; the third class suspension was from mid-July 2020 to late September 2020; and the fourth from mid-December 2020 until early March 2021. In mid-March 2021, schools reopened in stages. Before the Easter break, only one-third of students in each school were allowed to have face-to-face classes. After the Easter break, two-thirds of students in each school could resume normal lessons for a half-day timetable. The remaining students still had online lessons at home. From late May 2021 onwards, all students were back on campus to attend half-day classes.

If schools wanted to resume full-day classes, at least 80% of teaching staff and 70% of students in that school were required to be double vaccinated. Extracurricular activities were prohibited in compliance with the social distancing measure. Meanwhile, the fifth class suspension took place from mid-January 2022 until early May 2022 owing to the outbreak of a new Omicron coronavirus variant. At the time of writing, all schools could resume full-day classes owing to the cancellation of vaccine passes and the relinquishing of all social distancing measures.

Against this backdrop, remote teaching became indispensable. When the pandemic was rampant in 2021 and 2022, Hong Kong teachers adopted various forms of online teaching, be it synchronous (real-time video-conferencing classes) or asynchronous (pre-recorded lessons). For homework assignments, most schools utilised Google Classroom, OneNote or other common learning management systems to facilitate student learning despite the disruptions caused by multiple class suspensions. The schools of both Teacher A and Teacher B used Google Classroom as a default online learning platform. Because Teacher A and Teacher B were new to e-Portfolios, our team invited them to join the project by trying out e-Portfolios to see whether this digital tool could help consolidate their instructional practices and facilitate technology integration during class suspension.

Instruments

For this 1.5-year case study, our research team adopted three instruments to address two issues under study: technology integration and affordances/constraints experienced by teachers for this integration. These instruments included semi-structured interviews, classroom observations and reflective journals. The interview protocol was validated in a pilot study before the main study was carried out two years ago. The qualitative data were collected between July 2020 and December 2021. Our team conducted three semi-structured interviews with Teacher A and Teacher B individually. We observed both of their virtual classes twice in May 2020 and December 2021. Near the end of the study, we invited Teacher A and Teacher B to compose a 1500-word reflective journal on their own for the purpose of qualitative data collection and professional development. Albeit not the focus of this study, our team also interviewed the students of Teacher A and Teacher B in groups of three and four, respectively, and asked about their likes and dislikes of e-Portfolio compilation and what they benefited after constructing their e-Portfolios. Students' interview data were mainly used to deepen our research insights into this study. Concerning data analysis, the teachers' interview and observation data were transcribed for inductive and deductive analysis. Their reflective journals were coded by looking into what affordances and barriers they faced when integrating e-Portfolios into remote teaching. Three sources of data were constantly compared and contrasted throughout the study.

Integration

Teacher A: Al (pseudonym)

Al initiated his e-Portfolio programme by following the school policy. The principal set up Google Classroom as a *de facto* teaching and learning platform during the first and second waves of the pandemic. In Al's school, students and teachers used Google Classroom to submit and grade homework assignments, respectively (Inter[1]). Al thought that Google Classroom was mainly utilised as a homework storage space, which kept students' digital files for marking more than for learning (Inter). Hence, he decided to turn Google Classroom into an interactive instructional platform by changing his instructional approaches and engaging students in various learning tasks more proactively. During remote instruction, Al felt that he had less interaction with the students although he included learning games (Kahoot!) and question-and-answer sessions in each lesson (Obv). He was also concerned with missed contact hours, because he could not see his students every day by returning marked assignments to them and giving them verbal feedback (Inter).

After joining this case study, Al understood that e-Portfolios were synchronous, feedback-rich and interactive. To take advantage of these learning-orientated attributes, Al decided to innovate process writing with e-Portfolio tools to help his students master the target genre – argumentative essays, one of the most frequently tested genres in the school-leaving exam (Obv & Inter). When adopting the process writing approach, he required students to compose one brief paragraph after each lesson. Students were then provided with peer and teacher feedback before they resubmitted the revised paragraphs on their e-Portfolios the following day (Obv). Asked why he innovated process writing, Al said that he wanted to cater for learning diversity as most of his students were weak in academic writing (e.g. creating compelling arguments; Inter). Additionally, Al provided students with step-by-step scaffolding in writing alongside timely and individual feedback. By so doing, he could check on students' learning progress simultaneously (Obv). This kind of frequent monitoring facilitated Al in upholding the quality of instruction albeit switched to the online teaching mode unpredictably.

During another e-Portfolio lesson, in order to maximise virtual classroom dynamics, Al used chat rooms to elicit responses as some students remained reticent to speak up, preferring to type their answers on screen. He then utilised breakout rooms efficiently by dividing the class into pairs and groups of three only, so that students had ample opportunities to interact with one another. On one of his PowerPoint presentations, Al included educational hyperlinks such as a YouTube clip to explain what a restaurant review was, and a few dictionary entries of new vocabulary items to be learnt. His PowerPoint slides were informative and multimodal. Further, Al made interactive use of the shared screen function by deconstructing the schematic structure of an argumentative essay with multi-coloured annotations (Obv).

In addition to these functional changes made to the e-Portfolio platform, Al returned marked assignments to students within 48 hours through WhatsApp – an instance of timely feedback (Inter). An online feedback session was then arranged to debrief students' strengths and weaknesses in their paragraph writing (Obv). In one post-writing task featuring multi-drafting, Al encouraged students to compose a rebuttal collaboratively using Google Docs, in which they could edit and rewrite the draft synchronously or asynchronously (Inter). In brief, Al moderately integrated educational technology into his process-orientated writing instruction by substituting Zoom classes for in-person lessons with a few functional improvements, such as increased interactions and task engagement. He satisfactorily utilised a free messaging app to provide students with timely e-feedback and redesigned a post-writing task as an online collaborative writing task.

Teacher B: Bo (pseudonym)

Bo's school adopted Google Classroom as an e-Portfolio tool to help students organise and access their learning materials during class suspensions. Initially, Bo required students to organise their e-Portfolios by topic, e.g. Grammar – Irregular Adverbs, Vocabulary – COVID-19 pandemic and Narrative Writing 2 (Inter). To comply with the whole-school policy, Bo's colleagues reminded her that she should ask students to organise their e-Portfolios by date (cycles), for instance, under Cycle 1 (3–11 September 2020 – Grammar Worksheet 1 and Reading Comprehension 1; Inter). Initially, Bo thought that her students might find it easier to retrieve their learning tasks by date (cycles). However, near the end of the term, the students had information overload, since too many learning materials were uploaded onto Google Classroom and were not sorted by task type but by date. Bo added that her students' e-Portfolio contents were somewhat prescriptive, heavily bounded by the scheme of work assigned by the English panel chair (Inter).

Prior to this case study, Bo had not heard about e-Portfolios. After joining our study, she knew that e-Portfolios were likened to a record of students' learning progress (Inter). To prepare her junior form students for using e-Portfolios more proficiently, Bo provided them with a briefing session on how to upload and download files for homework submission and collection, respectively (Obv). She also taught students to convert a Word file into a PDF file for uploading. She admitted that she spared a few lessons to teach students how to arrange their learning materials according to designated dates (cycles) properly (Obv). Bo claimed that it took her a lot of time to help students manage their e-Portfolio artefacts. After familiarising herself with the logistics, Bo incorporated some e-learning materials such as online quizzes, Google Forms and topic-based reading passages into Google Classroom to facilitate flipped teaching (Inter).

When conducting remote teaching, Bo was concerned with reduced opportunities to interact with students and to provide timely feedback to students. To make up for the loss, she employed an app 'Explain Everything' together with iPad annotations to deliver blackboard-like instruction on Zoom. Bo also used the app 'Motability' in order to maximise virtual classroom interactions (Obv). Regardless of these technologies, in one of her online classes, Bo taught countable and uncountable nouns and some vocabulary items about the COVID-19 pandemic. The online lesson was contextualised and highly efficient, but Bo did not enhance classroom interactions by encouraging students to utilise the chat room and breakout room functions (Obv). Bo's online instruction was very similar to face-to-face instruction. She mainly adopted a lock-step approach, giving a mini-lecture on how to distinguish countable and uncountable nouns in a fill-in-the-blank reading task. Bo also told us that she preferred providing handwritten feedback rather than typing comments on Google Forms, as she was unable to circle students' errors and to provide more elaborated comments (Inter).

Although Bo was competent in using apps and Google Classroom, she did little to innovate her online teaching approach (Obv). Her instructional approach remained teacher centred and grammar focused, mainly following the scheme of work (Obv). In fact, she still struggled whether to instruct her students to arrange their e-Portfolio contents by 'task type' or by 'date' because she did not buy into the latter (Inter). In short, as compared to Al, Bo minimally integrated educational technology into her online teaching by substituting Zoom classes for face-to-face classes due to school closure, and modestly utilised iPad apps as a substitute for a physical whiteboard. In addition, Bo neither enhanced classroom dynamics efficiently, especially student–student interactions, nor provided detailed feedback to students using the synchronised functions of e-Portfolio platforms, including forums, chats and alert systems.

Affordances

For affordances, three themes were identified: (a) beliefs, (b) computer literacy and (c) user-friendliness of e-Portfolio tools. In (a), both Al and Bo were motivated to innovate the e-Portfolio approach despite their heavy workload and commitments. After all, this case study was voluntary. More importantly, they believed that e-Portfolios could help enhance students' learning during class suspensions, given that students could manipulate the e-Portfolio platform (i.e. Google Classroom accounts) properly (Inter). Al considered that he could innovate process writing in remote teaching with digital technology. He affirmed that as long as he was willing to shift his instructional approach, he could attempt process writing by harnessing the affordances of the e-Portfolio platform, e.g. high accessibility to students' work, quick turnaround time for feedback and more interactions for peer learning (Jour[2]). Although Bo's students were still learning how to organise their e-Portfolio artefacts, she trusted that e-Portfolios were likely to help them keep track of their learning if they could retrieve the right artefacts for review (Inter). Also, Bo was positive about e-Portfolio pedagogy because she could upload useful learning materials before each virtual lesson. Uploading pre-lesson preparation tasks definitely helped facilitate flipped teaching (Jour).

In (b), besides teacher beliefs, Al's and Bo's computer literacy levels would have an edge when they innovated e-Portfolios in their classroom contexts. Compared with Bo, Al appeared to be less confident in manipulating the interface of Google Classroom. Al admitted that he consulted his university friends regarding how to make pedagogical use of Zoom, Google Meet and Microsoft Teams in order to deliver his online classes more smoothly (Inter). Al was mainly self-taught when trying out various digital technologies. On the contrary, Bo had sound knowledge about specific learning apps (e.g. Motability) and selected learning management systems. She was particularly proficient in using iPad apps during remote teaching (Jour). She considered herself a tech-savvy teacher in the interview and reflective journal. Although Bo did not demonstrate a high level of technology integration when utilising e-Portfolios, her computer literacy level remained beneficial to future integration of e-learning and/or e-assessment initiatives (i.e. an instance of affordances of educational technology).

In (c), as to user-friendliness, Al and Bo felt that Google Classroom, adopted as an e-Portfolio tool, was easy to operate and manage, especially for collecting and grading homework assignments, although some students initially experienced difficulties in uploading and 'submitting' their work properly (Inter). Al added that the inclusion of other components of Google Suite into Google Classroom could facilitate remote teaching productively, such as online quizzes (Google Forms), collaborative tasks (Google Docs) and synchronous communications (Google Meet; Jour). While the e-Portfolio platform was relatively easy to manipulate, Al said that he was still learning new functions, such as how students could navigate and curate multimodal artefacts to perform self-reflection (Inter). Bo also concurred that Google Classroom was flexible and accessible compared with other learning management systems such as Moodle. However, she was concerned with its usefulness when teachers wanted to include some constructed response assessment tasks as the interface of Google Classroom might restrict short essay-type answers (Inter).

Constraints

For constraints, three themes were identified: (1) the provision of information technology (IT) support, (2) a testing culture and (3) the integration of e-Portfolios into curricula. In (1), Al and Bo claimed that their schools did not offer any proper IT training for teachers when face-to-face teaching switched to remote teaching (Inter). As said before, Al was mainly self-taught when he learnt how to manipulate the e-Portfolio platform Google Classroom. Bo acquired the technical know-how about learning apps and Google Classroom prior to remote teaching. Both said that their schools were somewhat slow in responding to the sudden shift to online teaching during the first wave of the pandemic (Jour). Because of a clear lack of IT support and ambiguous homework policies, the two teachers initially found it very perplexing to guide students to manage their e-Portfolio accounts. Fortunately, Al's and Bo's schools provided every student with an iPad for home-based learning (Inter). A similar support mechanism has been reported in Cheung's (2021) case study. Apparently, the inadequate provision of IT training and infrastructure during and after the pandemic was a cause for concern because not every school had adequate resources to allow teachers and students access to free-of-charge electronic gadgets.

In (2), despite having autonomy to innovate e-Portfolios, Al and Bo had less control over the e-Portfolio contents because both were expected to closely comply with the scheme of work of their respective grade levels and the public exam syllabus (Inter). According to the two teachers, the schemes of work remained top-down and prescriptive, rendering little space for them to explore useful contents for e-Portfolio compilation. For instance, Al tried out process writing with Google Classroom, but his teaching content remained restrictive to the most frequently tested genre that appeared in the school leaving exam – argumentative essays (Jour). In our observations, Bo only taught what was assessed in the forthcoming uniform test – adverbs of place, time and manner. Her instructional approach largely emphasised drilling, namely the robotic use of fill in the blanks, short answer questions or yes-no questions during online lessons. It appears that a larger exam-driven culture might have inhibited how the two teachers promoted creativity and metacognitive thinking in the e-Portfolio compilation process.

In (3), although e-Portfolios were essential rather than optional during class suspensions, Al and Bo found that when schools reopened after suspension, students stopped using their e-Portfolios (Jour). They wondered whether this alternative tool could be sustained when the pandemic was under control and in-person classes resumed for good, especially when all social distancing and quarantine restrictions were lifted. Al and Bo felt that since most colleagues regarded formative e-Portfolio compilation as an *ad hoc* learning event, they might marginalise its integration into the mainstream curriculum when full-day school resumed in the near future (Inter). If e-Portfolio pedagogy was denied as a legitimate status, its wider application was less likely to be successful. Also, because Al and Bo were occupied with heavy teaching and administrative duties, implementing e-Portfolios during their remote or later face-to-face instruction would become a burden if this digital tool was not seamlessly integrated into the existing L2 curriculum.

Discussion

Based upon the above data, three post-pandemic lessons learnt from the case study were identified: (1) modifying language pedagogy via technology; (2) shifting summative to formative purposes of assessment; and (3) creating a critical mass of colleagues for integration.

Modifying language pedagogy with technology

In addition to adopting e-Portfolios as a direct substitute for remote instruction, teachers ought to adjust their instructional approaches to accommodate learners' diverse needs. In Al's lessons, although the students could not compose a full-length essay in one go, he tried out process writing in order to help them write one brief paragraph with online peer and teacher feedback. This pedagogical modification enables less-able students to compose a piece of argumentative essay after several attempts and utilises the functions of e-Portfolio software to the full, namely the retrieval of timely written e-feedback and the benefits of virtual collaborative writing via Google Docs (an instance of integration). Without altering his online instructional approach, Al was unsuccessful in innovating process writing with the e-Portfolio platform. In Bo's lessons, although she was confident in applying educational technologies, she merely used Google Classroom as a direct substitute for a physical homework submission and collection method. Bo used certain iPad apps to enhance virtual classroom interactions in her lessons without much success because she did not change her instructional approach fundamentally, namely from a lockstep, teacher-centred approach to a more bottom-up, student-centred approach. Since Bo relied heavily on teacher–student interactions in her online lessons, the students hardly had any opportunity to collaborate with one another. In our case study, the level of technology integration depended on the extent to which teachers could transform and contextualise their online pedagogical approaches to suit the virtual learning environment in various e-Portfolio platforms (Cheung, 2021; Hockly & Dudeney, 2018).

Shifting summative to formative purpose of assessment

In line with the published e-Portfolio research, both teacher informants primarily used e-Portfolios for the summative purpose of assessment, e.g. grading students' daily homework assignments. Apart from providing students with synchronised and asynchronised feedback, Al and Bo did not make full use of the learning-orientated potentials of e-Portfolios to support students' L2 learning. From the data, the two teachers did not encourage their students to create and curate multimodal learning evidence when uploading their assignments, such as audio files, video files or augmented reality artefacts other than text files. Undeniably, mobilising students to compile multimedia learning artefacts empowered them to be creative, independent and computer literate (Yancey, 2019). In addition, Al and Bo did not invite students to review their learning periodically and metacognitively. After all, reflection is a key feature of paper-based and digital portfolios that allow students to learn how to set goals, review learning with feedback and adjust learning for enhancement accordingly (Aygün & Aydin, 2016). Helping students to set up e-Portfolios as a digital dossier and a learning place is the first step. Redirecting students' efforts in fulfilling the formative purpose of e-Portfolios such as active engagement in self-assessment and peer review is the second, because e-Portfolios were originally designed to support learning rather than to evaluate learning (Barrett, 2010; Lam, 2020). On the assessment front, the two teachers are said to integrate technology very minimally to achieve the formative purpose of assessment through e-Portfolio software. Similar to other teachers who attempt e-Portfolios, they need to develop a deeper conceptual understanding of what formative assessment entails and how best e-Portfolios can fulfil the formative purpose of assessment to enhance student learning in L2 classroom settings (Gu & Lam, 2023; Walland & Shaw, 2022).

Creating a critical mass of colleagues for integration

To integrate e-Portfolios into teaching, principals can consider creating a critical mass of colleagues to support technology integration. Principals and school senior management can encourage the use of e-Portfolios as a whole-school approach on the resumption of face-to-face classes. Working in teams would definitely lessen teachers' stress and anxiety when they innovate e-Portfolios as one prevailing form of remote teaching. Even for in-person classes, principals should allow teachers to conduct up to 10%–20% of online lessons in a semester for the sake of integrating flipped teaching. In our case study, Al and Bo worked in isolation when trying out the e-Portfolio method. Research has shown that without a critical mass, technology integration such as e-Portfolios is doomed to failure because such integration could not be duly expanded and then sustained (Eynon & Gambino, 2017). Not surprisingly, Al and Bo experienced numerous individual and institutional constraints. To promote technology integration, principals and ministries of education could step up L2 teachers' professional training in information and communication technology (ICT) and e-Portfolio pedagogy because Al and Bo reported that they received no formal training when face-to-face classes abruptly shifted to emergent remote teaching (Cooper *et al.*, 2022). By having more computer-literate teachers, they can form a critical mass when piloting, developing and innovating e-Portfolio programmes to deliver remote instruction within a community of practice. The opportunity for collegial collaboration is a way forward to e-Portfolio integration now that in-person teaching has restarted (Lam, 2023).

Pedagogical Implications

This section unfolds two pedagogical implications: (1) a call for teacher e-Portfolio literacy and (2) an inquiry into teacher beliefs. These two implications are likely to facilitate e-Portfolio integration in L2 settings. From the two case scenarios, Al appears to integrate e-Portfolios into his L2 instruction to a larger extent than Bo, because Bo, albeit tech-savvy, lacks e-Portfolio literacy to support fuller technology integration. Also, both teachers' technology integration was obviously influenced by their idiosyncratic belief systems. E-Portfolio literacy entails teachers' knowledge, skills and awareness when teachers use e-Portfolios or other related digital instructional tools in their work contexts. The construct includes a complex interplay of conceptual rationale, expertise, logistics, applications, affordances, constraints and a host of related dimensions, such as the fairness, impacts and sustainability of e-Portfolio pedagogy and assessment (Tsagari, 2021). The acquisition of e-Portfolio literacy entails a plethora of good formative assessment practices, namely the provision of instant and revisable e-feedback, the adoption of multimodal feedback to close learning gaps and the promotion of self-regulated learning strategies through the functions of various e-Portfolio software applications or learning management systems (Bakla, 2020; Ene & Upton, 2018). As to teacher beliefs, prior research on technology integration has largely emphasised the technical aspects of applying technology into classroom teaching, such as teacher knowledge and skills (Fabian & Topping, 2019) and how institutional factors may impede their integration (Meyer *et al.*, 2011). However, scholars have overlooked the importance of teacher beliefs or cognition regarding why teachers preferred adopting one e-Portfolio function over another (e.g. curating artefacts in Al's case vs organising artefacts in Bo's class) or why they innovated their instruction in writing rather than speaking through e-Portfolios. Without looking into teacher beliefs and cognition, scholars never understand why teachers integrate e-Portfolios into their language instruction and what intended purposes they want to fulfil, especially during the pandemic and thereafter (Farrell & Stanclik, 2021).

Summary

Chapter 7 reported on a case study about e-Portfolio integration. It then presented how the pandemic has transformed the remote teaching landscape globally. The chapter went on to describe the details of the study, namely design, informants, context, instruments and data analysis. The findings section showed how two teacher informants adopted e-Portfolios to deliver L2 teaching virtually during the pandemic, and how they encountered affordances and constraints throughout the integration process. Afterwards, three post-pandemic lessons derived from the case study were discussed, namely modifying language pedagogy via technology, shifting summative to formative purposes of assessment and creating a critical mass of colleagues for integration. The chapter ended with two teaching implications, which facilitated technology integration by increasing teacher e-Portfolio literacy and understanding teacher beliefs.

Notes

(1) 'Inter' stands for interview data and 'Obv' stands for observation data.
(2) 'Jour' stands for teacher reflective journals.

8 Applications of e-Portfolio Tools: Commentary

Introduction

Chapter 8 reviews common e-Portfolio application tools and provides readers with a description of each tool. First, it introduces four categories of e-Portfolio tools, which are extensively adopted in second language (L2) classrooms. It then evaluates these tools with major dimensions of technological innovations. The chapter subsequently discusses issues arising from the wider implementation of these e-Portfolio tools. The penultimate section presents an in-depth commentary on six of the most up-to-date e-Portfolio tools in terms of aims, target users, functionality, instructional merits and drawbacks, as well as practicality.

Types of e-Portfolio Tools

In language education, scholars can categorise four major software e-Portfolio tools: (a) self-authoring tools (e.g. a suite of Microsoft 365 software programmes); (b) interactive web services (e.g. common Web 2.0 applications); (c) commercial e-Portfolio software tools (e.g. Mahara); and (d) social media (i.e. social networking sites; Lam, 2021a). In (a), self-authoring tools encourage students to create textual, arithmetic, graphic and presentation content via a range of software programmes, such as Microsoft Word, Excel, OneNote and PowerPoint. These programmes can be freely downloaded from students' institutions or accessed by subscriptions. In (b), common Web 2.0 applications refer to a virtual learning environment, where students create and share content online and offline. Prominent examples of these tools are wiki (i.e. WikiHow, WikiBooks), weblogs (i.e. Bloggers, WordPress) and podcasts. In (c), commercial e-Portfolio software alludes to custom-made learning management systems that provide a digital space for students to document their language learning in a systematic way. From primary to junior secondary school contexts, Seesaw and FreshGrade are, thus far, the most popular e-Portfolio tools among others. In (d), more and more scholars and teachers utilise social media, such as Facebook and Instagram, as an e-Portfolio platform to help students improve their academic writing (Barrot, 2021). The following section evaluates the usefulness of these four categories of e-Portfolio tools in terms of multimodality, mobility, instantaneous participation and interactivity.

Aspects of Technological Innovation

Self-authoring tools enable students to create multimodal artefacts by inserting hyperlinks, audios and/or vlogs on OneNote pages or PowerPoint presentations. Concerning mobility, these tools can be used anywhere as long as a stable internet connection is available. Instantaneous participation would be a disadvantage because utilising these self-authoring tools may not necessarily be synchronous, especially when students are offline. Content creators and users are not in sync with one another in real time unlike other tools. Likewise, interactivity may be a cause for concern since these tools are not intended for communal sharing unless those artefacts (i.e. word processing files or presentation slideshows) are uploaded to learning management systems (Yancey, 2009).

Interactive web services offer different spectrums. First, they are web based in nature and can easily host multimedia artefacts with large file sizes and multiple formats. Second, Web 2.0 applications can be accessed by different operating systems and gadgets at any time. Third, albeit not synchronous at all times, weblogs and wikis allow users to provide peer response. These dynamic tools promote instantaneous participation although not as speedy as instant messaging apps, such as WeChat or WhatsApp (Navarre, 2019). In terms of interactivity, weblogs and podcasts could reach a wider community and disseminate e-Portfolio content quicker, since they assist students to publish their works online.

Commercial e-Portfolio software tools are technically designed for hosting multimodal artefacts. Mobility is an edge as most e-Portfolio tools can be easily accessed through mobile apps, laptops, desktops and tablets to accommodate students' learning needs in different locales. Some tools include a family version, so that parents can get involved in their children's learning (Moorhouse & Beaumont, 2020). Most e-Portfolio software tools facilitate instantaneous participation through their announcement systems. In Seesaw and Schoology, the submission of homework assignments and the provision of online peer/teacher feedback alert students almost instantly. Interactivity remains restricted to school–family contexts because publishing students' digital artefacts via e-Portfolios needs teachers' and parents' consent (Osorio-Saez *et al.*, 2021).

More recently, adopting social media as e-Portfolio platforms has become a trend. Social media-based e-Portfolios enhance multimodality because their interfaces support the public sharing of image-based and video-based artefacts. As students and teachers mainly access social networking sites via smartphones, social media-based e-Portfolios have high mobility. L2 learning via these platforms can take place inside and outside classrooms. Instantaneous participation is not an issue for social media-based e-Portfolios as these sites promote social presence, information sharing and group participation in a virtual environment (Lee, 2022). Facebook- and Instagram-based e-Portfolios facilitate interactivity among peer–peer, peer–teacher, teacher–peer and teacher–parent communications by 'liking', 'sharing', 'following' and 'posting comments' functions (Purnama, 2017). The next section discusses relevant issues arising from the application of e-Portfolio tools in L2 environments.

Issues Arising from the Application of e-Portfolio Tools

Based upon the scholarship from e-learning and e-Portfolios in education, Stefani *et al.* (2007) pointed out that some issues remain unresolved and unclear to researchers and teachers when e-Portfolios are put into practice, including reflection, evidence, multimedia components and multiple presentations.

Reflection

Scholars question whether e-Portfolio software programmes comprise a reflective element or student reflection practices, given that some tools are simply adopted as a digital dossier for students to submit and collect their homework assignments online (Zheng & Barrot, 2022). In other words, these e-Portfolio programmes render students content suppliers rather than active agents who compile, curate and review their digital artefacts to improve their language learning. Additionally, although teachers require students to self-reflect upon their artefacts to enhance learning, they may not guarantee that students can engage in a deep level of reflection, especially when they lack explicit training in this aspect. Likewise, teachers may find it taxing to teach students how to perform self-reflection and self-assessment, as developing a capacity to reflect is considered tacit knowledge and intangible procedures in L2 instruction (Teng & Zhang, 2022).

Evidence

For reflection, researchers raised concern about how students could curate and link digital artefacts as evidence of language learning to justify their self-reflection on various e-Portfolio tools. Lam (2022c) identified that students often selected representative works to showcase their L2 learning without knowing or justifying the rationale. Thus, they simply chose an artefact by intuition or by coincidence. Worse still, these students usually chose a wrong piece of evidence to support their self-reflection, not to mention those who did not know how to make an informed decision on linking learning, evidence and reflection by proper validation (i.e. triangulating e-Portfolio data with reflection statements individually or collectively). Belgrad (2013) long suggested that creating a culture of evidence was crucial in e-Portfolio-based contexts because those digital tools allowed students to acquire metacognitive capacities by curating, self-assessing and showcasing evidence of learning recursively.

Multimedia components

While nearly all e-Portfolio tools can store multimodal artefacts, it appears that students primarily upload text-based artefacts as one staple source of homework assignments. In fact, teachers should encourage students to create audios, videos or a blend of still pictures, clips, music and texts (i.e. digital storytelling) that capture their L2 learning trajectories more dependably (Sun & Yang, 2015). Teachers may also guide students to view and comment on their classmates' digital artefacts as formative peer assessment. With that said, archiving multimedia components in e-Portfolio tools requires fundamental skills to upload, display and organise artefacts to achieve both the learning and grading functions of assessment. Hence, digital multimodal composing should be taught explicitly in project-based learning or task-based English curricula, so that students are fully equipped with the capacity to curate and review multimodal artefacts in e-Portfolio software tools for an authentic purpose (Cheung, 2022).

Multiple presentations

Multiple presentations refer to the frequency and number of e-Portfolios that students are expected to develop. If e-Portfolios are used at the course or programme level, students may construct one per semester or per school year. When teachers adopt a whole-school approach to e-Portfolio pedagogy, students are required to construct one entirely for either primary or secondary schooling (Stefani et al., 2007). Additionally, teachers need to identify which e-Portfolio tools best facilitate interdisciplinary, experiential and extracurricular learning, and the extent to which these tools can transfer multimodal artefacts from one platform to another. After all, multiple presentations of e-Portfolios for L2 learning possibly diminish their sustainability and practicality. When selecting e-Portfolio tools, teachers should take the purpose of e-Portfolio programmes into consideration, such as project-based, personal or institutional ones, because some tools are designed for school settings while some for personal use (Karlin et al., 2016). The next section presents a comprehensive commentary on individual e-Portfolio tools.

Commentary on e-Portfolio Tools

This section reviews six common e-Portfolio software tools in accordance with their aims, target users, functions, instructional merits and drawbacks, and practicality. The tools under review include Google Classroom (https://classroom.google.com/), Microsoft Teams (https:// teams.microsoft.com/), Schoology (https://app.schoology.com/), Near- pod (https://nearpod.com/), Anthology Portfolio (https://www.anthology .com/material/portfolio) and Instagram (https://www.instagram.com/).

Google Classroom

Thus far, Google Classroom is one of the most common virtual learning environments that facilitate remote instruction, blended learn- ing and assignment management on- and off-campus. More importantly, the software is free and has an education version (Google Workspace for Education) primarily created for online learning in compulsory educa- tion settings. Although originally designed for submitting, distributing and organising homework assignments online, Google Classroom can be utilised as an e-Portfolio tool as it entails the elements of creation, curation, revision and circulation. The component of *revision* may be tricky because not all teachers require students to review, reflect upon and revise their artefacts for the learning-orientated purpose. The target user ranges from Grade 3 to post-secondary level.

The function of Google Classroom is for teachers to manage online classes; to assign homework with clear instructions and rubrics; and to conduct remote teaching via Google Meet. Teachers can create a Google Classroom on any default template, assign tasks and make announce- ments in the same interface. They then assign students to complete in- class exercises or homework tasks with due dates, guidelines, assessment weightings and rubrics. Teachers may save these marked assignments for whole-class debriefing or one-on-one conferencing whenever neces- sary. Starting in 2021, teachers can conduct online lessons, conferences or extra tutorials using Google Meet (a video-conferencing tool powered by Google) within the same Google Classroom. Additionally, teach- ers can apply a suite of software programmes, such as Google Drive (a cloud-based storage system), Docs (an online word processor), Forms (an online survey), Sheets, Slides, Sites (a collaborative online learning hub) and Gmail together with Google Classroom to facilitate synchronous interactions and virtual communications.

Concerning its merits, Google Classroom is all-in-one, easy to use, collaborative and highly accessible. Teachers can bring in all the learning tools to facilitate their instructional approaches and, at the same time, manage multiple classes in one central platform. Google Classroom is somewhat user-friendly. Its interface is sufficiently straightforward for teachers to set up a virtual classroom and invite students to join by using QR codes or emails. With Google Docs, teachers can work with stu- dents simultaneously in the same document. Teachers can promote peer assessment and collaborative writing via Google Docs. Through Google

Meet, teachers and students can have dialogues whenever clarifications are needed. More importantly, these Google learning apps and websites are easily accessed using mainstream operating systems, such as Android- and iOS-supported mobile devices. As to drawbacks, Google Classroom lacks a built-in gradebook and automated quizzes. Although teachers can assign numerical scores (e.g. 100%) on tasks set in Google Forms, as of yet there is no standard-referenced grading option. Teachers need to compose qualitative comments to justify the marks they have given.

Speaking of practicality, Google Classroom is relatively simple to set up, maintain and expand its pedagogical function. For instance, by adding the learning app Kami (https://www.kamiapp.com/) to Google Classroom, teachers can grade students' portfolio work and return it without logging out of the tool. For formative assessment, Kami has a 'real-time responding system', so that student–teacher interactions can be made instantaneous. It further provides students with personalised feedback by utilising screen captures, voice and video comments to increase engagement. For summative assessment, teachers can grade multiple assignments simultaneously using the 'grade-by-page' function and recycling standardised comments from the 'annotation bank' to expedite scoring procedures. To support learner diversity, teachers can assign tasks with various levels of difficulty to students in Google Classroom. As mentioned, Google Meet has recently merged with Google Classroom. Teachers could make use of some newly added features of Google Meet, including Q&A, polling, breakout room, hand-raising and attendance checking to keep students actively engaged in remote classes. Furthermore, teachers may create digital exit tickets as a post-lesson formative assessment exercise for students to review their language learning independently.

Microsoft Teams

Like Google Classroom, Microsoft Teams is one of the most popular and free-of-charge collaboration and learning management systems. It is used with the Office 365 Suite, including Microsoft Word, Excel, PowerPoint, OneNote, OneDrive, Forms, plus some other non-Microsoft tools. Its aim is to promote the co-creation of a virtual learning community via shared digital resources (files and apps), chat sessions, online classes/meetings and synchronic collaborations. Microsoft Teams is a good fit as an e-Portfolio tool because it has multiple software programmes to help showcase students' linguistic competence, namely textual, audio, algorithmic and presentational tools. Its target user ranges from Grade 5 to tertiary-level students. However, Microsoft Teams might not be an option for younger learners, especially those aged 10 or below, as its interface is more technically sophisticated than that of Google Classroom.

The role of Microsoft Teams is threefold. First, it facilitates online collaboration among internal (peers and teachers) and external community members (the public) instantaneously via phone calls, live chats and file sharing. Second, it helps teachers organise and manage a virtual classroom by putting instructional materials in place, such as e-books, hyperlinks for listening tasks, quizzes, writing exercises and audios of solo/group presentations. Third, Microsoft Teams enables teachers to provide timely formative feedback and teach various language skills holistically in remote or blended instruction by syncing with two tools – Whiteboard.chat (https://www.whiteboard.chat/) and immersive reader in Word. The former tool helps teachers to observe, support and collaborate with students' language learning by providing individual scaffolding to each student whenever they see fit. The latter tool helps students acquire intensive reading skills via hearing a text read aloud (English pronunciation), analysing different 'parts of speech' (grammar patterns) and utilising a 'picture dictionary' (vocabulary). These functions can make e-Portfolio instruction learning orientated and technologically fulfilling.

The benefits of using Microsoft Teams as an e-Portfolio tool include collaboration and compatibility. The software supports students, teachers, educators and parents to meet, get together, create content and share resources remotely via Office 365 Education. Such a collaborative pedagogical mode dovetails with the attribute of e-Portfolio instruction. Furthermore, because of the all-powerful ecosystem of Teams software, it is compatible with many third-party learning apps or tools, which provide teachers with opportunities to liven up their instructional approaches and cater for learning diversity. Despite these merits, Microsoft Teams has limitations. It is considered less user-friendly than other tools because its interface is not easy for students. Teachers may need specific training on how the features of Teams and other Office 365 software can be integrated to create a one-stop language lesson. The free version of Teams can only house up to 300 students in one meeting. The shared storage size of the free version is also restricted to 10 GB and cloud-based storage for individual users to 2 GB.

Generally, Microsoft Teams has high practicality because it syncs with both Microsoft and non-Microsoft learning tools. Teachers can create, assign and grade individual, group or class assignments formatively with interactive experiences by adding some classroom-friendly tools such as Pear Deck (https://www.peardeck.com/microsoft). Likewise, by using a shared OneNote Class Notebook, teachers can deliver instructional materials via the 'Content Library', work with students synchronously through 'Collaboration Space' and provide students with private feedback (recorded audios). More importantly, the OneNote Class Notebook can be used as an interactive whiteboard that helps teachers conduct remote instruction effectively. While Microsoft Teams has the potential to rival Google Classroom or Schoology, teachers may find it complicated to navigate on its platform, which is not as intuitive as some other tools. Initially, teachers could consider creating worksheets, monitoring students' learning progress or utilising collaborative whiteboards for online teaching to familiarise themselves with the basic features of the tool before they experience other advanced functions.

Schoology

Schoology is a cloud-based learning management system that can be used as a student digital dossier for the compilation and curation of multimodal artefacts. This digital tool is conveniently synced with any school information systems to enable class teachers to manage their classes remotely and to conduct blended instruction seamlessly. The aim of Schoology is to create coursework content, promote group work, share instructional resources (i.e. e-books, hyperlinks and useful databanks), do roll calls, assign homework and grade students' work with e-feedback. Schoology is likened to a social networking site but with a focus on language/subject learning. Like its counterparts, Schoology can be used with similar personal cloud-based devices (Dropbox, https://www.dropbox.com/ or Google Drive) and a note-taking plus learning management app (i.e. Evernote, https://evernote.com/intl/zh-tw). Its target users are K-12 students.

To support online or face-to-face instruction, Schoology performs three functions: (a) management of course materials, (b) creation of multimedia assignments and (c) tracking of student learning. In (a), teachers can arrange teaching and coursework materials to suit their pedagogical styles, namely arranging resources by language skills, topical themes, months or objectives. The collapsible folder design keeps each page neat and coordinated. In (b), Schoology enables teachers to generate a wide range of assessment types (i.e. 18), such as answers to questions set on course readings, uploads of video clips or audios, discussion posts, online quizzes and multimedia project files. These assessment tasks can be stored as a student's portfolio in the tool. In (c), to monitor learning, Schoology includes a built-in gradebook that allows teachers to grade by numerical scores or percentages. Teachers can align course/programme objectives with each question or assessment item to track students' mastery of language learning. Some assignments could be set for automated grading, so that students are likely to develop autonomy and self-awareness of their learning trajectories.

The merits of Schoology are twofold. First, it has multiple pedagogical features that enrich teachers' instructional repertoires. The digital tool is an enabling platform for skill extension, content scaffolding and time management, especially for senior secondary-level students who may be more computer literate to navigate its interface. Second, the platform is ideal for designing formative assessment tasks. Teachers may upload textual, video or audio instructions for homework assignments. Younger learners and less-able students can audio-record their questions if they are unclear about certain instructions. To promote formative assessment, teachers can provide quick written or audio feedback with annotations and monitor students' learning progress using badges, gradebooks, email/app notifications and workload monitoring functions. Nevertheless, new users can, perhaps, feel overwhelmed with the multilayered interface of Schoology. It takes time for teachers to set up a learning-supported virtual classroom to suit their instructional styles and approaches. Students (i.e. junior ones) might need structured training in navigating different folders and pages, uploading artefacts and responding to e-feedback appropriately.

Schoology is moderately practical in terms of syncing with other digital tools. Recently, it has improved its technical integration with Google and Microsoft software programmes, so that teachers can create more innovative curricula to facilitate L2 teaching and learning. For instance, Google Slides or Docs are easily embedded into a class page of Schoology by simply 'cutting and pasting' a link from 'Publish Google Slides to web' to 'Schoology embed code'. Teachers can assign personalised homework tasks for each student whose educational needs are diverse. To enhance school–parent communications, teachers can create a parent- or grade-level chat group and post class activities and school announcements to regularly update parents on their child's progress. Teachers and school administrators can store important resources in group folders, so that everyone has access to them for wider sharing and dissemination. Although Schoology is free to individual teachers, schools and districts need to pay for value-added features to manage hundreds of users and different courses.

Nearpod

Nearpod is a powerful presentation tool that facilitates the delivery of interactive lessons in an online or face-to-face mode. Each lesson comprises multiple slide templates that support various formats of content, including videos, PDFs, webpages and built-in activities (i.e. matching pairs). The platform is designed for instructional presentations more than the management of learning artefacts, although the tool is compatible with other learning management systems such as Google Classroom and Schoology. The aim of the tool is to facilitate the creation of interactive lesson presentations, formative and summative assessments, and online/blended lessons delivery. Owing to its dynamic and formative nature, Nearpod is pedagogically appropriate for promoting classroom engagement and participation through in-class gaming activities and student-directed learning tasks in any e-Portfolio-based curriculum. Its target users range from kindergarten to post-secondary students.

As to functions, Nearpod can be used to deliver multimodal lessons, to increase classroom engagement and to conduct formative assessment tasks. For multimodal lessons, teachers can create original multimedia presentations or customise their instructional materials by drawing from the Nearpod Library. Teachers can upload videos, images, audios and digital files, and incorporate some virtual reality (VR) elements to expand their pedagogical strategies. For classroom engagement, the very attribute of Nearpod is to enhance teacher–student and student–student interactions via slideshow-based lessons. Teachers can adopt dynamic gamification and learner-centred activities, such as 'drag & drop', 'draw it', 'matching pairs', polling and multiple-choice questions to increase classroom dynamics. For formative assessment, Nearpod allows teachers to create a wide range of open-ended tasks to assess students' language learning. It invites students to self-assess their assignments by using polling to indicate how they could further improve their performances. Through some formative assessment activities such as quizzes and 'draw it' tasks, teachers can observe students' immediate responses and adjust their instructions on the fly.

There are three benefits to teachers using Nearpod as an e-Portfolio tool. First, teachers can give instant multimedia feedback to students for a quick learning review. Such spontaneity could greatly reduce classroom routines or assignment turnaround time. Second, students can raise questions via chats, take and annotate notes on 'Student Notes' and even learn a lesson at their own pace (i.e. selection of self-study mode: 'Student-Paced' banner). In other words, students are free to choose the instructional mode they prefer. Third, teachers and students are fully supported to engage in meaningful partnerships, interactions and discussions through polling, collaboration boards, quizzes and upvoting comments. Hence, Nearpod is ideally used for remote or blended instruction since its interactive features can foster virtual classroom communications. Yet, one limitation is that teachers need more time to proficiently manipulate the interface and functionalities of Nearpod because some functions are rather sophisticated. The tool perhaps needs to include a content filter to facilitate the retrieval of resources (i.e. cloud-based lesson templates) from a massive content library.

Nearpod is highly practical in terms of promoting classroom engagement and feedback literacy. The slideshow-based lessons encourage students to proactively engage in any L2 lessons by drawing on a map, posting a note on the collaboration board or participating in game-based learning. Teachers can help students to acquire key learning concepts and vocabulary items by incorporating Flocabulary (https://www.flocabulary.com/) videos into their presentations. To learn outside classrooms, teachers can use Nearpod's VR lessons to take students on a virtual field trip to a national park or an overseas country. For feedback literacy, students can receive and respond to multimodal e-feedback rapidly, so that they can understand, adopt and integrate pertinent feedback information into their works in progress for revision, especially for process writing and multistaged project work. Students also get ample opportunities to learn how to respond to peer and/or teacher comments in other medium, such as graphics, audios or videos.

Anthology Portfolio

Anthology Portfolio (formerly Chalk & Wire) is a web-based e-Portfolio tool combining a grading programme, a portfolio site and a learning management system. Since the tool was originally designed for student compilation and the curation of digital artefacts to showcase learning, its ecosystem is compatible with the attributes of e-Portfolio-based curricula and assessment. The tool is also a good fit for L2 teacher education because the platform can store lesson plans, observation data, teacher portfolios and school mentors' reports for summative evaluation against institutional requirements and state-wide professional standards. That said, Anthology Portfolio welcomes advanced L2 learners to self-assess their professional and experiential learning electronically. It aims to empower teachers to create criterion-referenced assessments, monitor student progress and provide feedback/grades to students for review. The target users of Anthology Portfolio are tertiary students.

Anthology Portfolio has several unique functions that link with the features of e-Portfolios. First, they capture the student learning journey through multiple sources of evidence. Like other tools, students can curate and adopt their assessment results as evidence of learning. Anthology Portfolio has robust feedback tools that allow students to review their assignments, reflect on learning, document skill development and highlight achievements efficiently. Second, they demonstrate student growth and improvement over time using analytics. Such an innovative technology enhances students' self-reflection for e-Portfolios with reliable assessment information. Third, they integrate well with other common learning management systems. With powerful import options, students can easily import multimedia artefacts from Google Drive or OneDrive to compile their e-Portfolios. Fourth, the tool supports students and faculties to develop their language skills and showcase their achievements with 'sharable portfolios'. This function facilitates a collaborative workspace. When students update their e-Portfolios, they can choose co-editors (their peers or the teacher) with whom to share their works in progress to elicit editorial and/or social learning support whenever necessary.

The merits of Anthology Portfolio include the provision of unlimited and customisable portfolio templates, easy goal and activity tracking, and enhanced experiential learning. Owing to their sophisticated design, Anthology Portfolio facilitates individualised and institutional e-Portfolio building processes. They provide wide-ranging and highly customised portfolio choices for students with different educational needs. Since Anthology Portfolio is an incarnation of continuous assessment, it assists students and teachers to track learning development. Students can translate their assessment results in the form of a graphical analysis and share them with admissions officers or prospective employers. Anthology Portfolio can also be utilised to enhance students' experiential learning, as the tool can help students to curate their off-campus learning artefacts in a sustainable manner. Nonetheless, Anthology Portfolio has minor drawbacks. As with certain software programmes designed for advanced students, the tool has a standard but not a user-friendly interface. Since the operation workflows may not be as intuitive as expected, students and faculties may need to refer to the user manual to manipulate some fundamental functions. Despite being professionally congruous with teacher and language education, Anthology Portfolio may not be very practical. As a system designed for tertiary education, Anthology Portfolio has integrated numerous advanced functions for performance tracking and profile building. These can only be purchased by institutions so individual teachers cannot use them in their work contexts for free. All operations of the tool need to be performed on the web. Other operating systems (i.e. Android or iOS apps) are currently not available for the e-Portfolio tool. Teacher and student users can access the registration and login page only through the portal of their respective institution. In other words, students cannot log in to the system separately from their university intranet account. Additionally, the system expects teacher and student users to have attained a certain level of computer literacy to proficiently navigate the interface.

Instagram

Instagram is a photo- and video-sharing social media app that features the instant dissemination of image-based post and video-based story content among followers. It has a photographic filter that helps to upgrade the quality of those uploaded images. Instagram was initially designed for social networking, marketing and digital advertising. It aims to build social networks with other users/followers via posts and/or live, to promote new products and manufacturers and to create spaces for entertainment via Reel and/or Instagram Story. In L2 education, Instagram can be adopted as an e-Portfolio tool to help students capture their language learning moments via the above functions, especially posts or reel. Those uploaded images or videos can be used as up-to-date learning evidence to showcase students' learning histories. The target users of Instagram are 12 and over.

Since Instagram is an image-based social media, students can use graphics and videos to support their learning. For instance, they may shoot a short clip together with pictures to create an Instagram Highlight to recount how they overcame certain aspects of L2 learning and invite peers to upvote or leave comments. To fully utilise the resources of digital environments on Instagram, students can adopt the hashtag function to build online spaces beyond their target users (i.e. to locate like-minded users who encountered similar challenges in L2 learning, say intelligibility of regional accents and issues in pronunciation). This function can also expand students' academic circles by sharing and negotiating how to master an L2. Another function of Instagram is that it increases student engagement in L2 learning by uploading and updating multimodal contents to enhance online interactions and collaboration. For example, students participate in preparing a book launch project collectively or conducting a mini research project by identifying the most intriguing Instagram storyteller with metrics and justifications.

Like other e-Portfolio tools, Instagram has merits and drawbacks. On the plus side, Instagram appeals to adolescent learners and young adults as its interface is chic. More importantly, Instagram is user-friendly and its basic functions are somewhat easy to manipulate. Second, Instagram is a mixture of other social media tools, including Facebook (social enticement), Reddit (photographic filters), X (formerly Twitter; hashtags and followers) and YouTube (likes and commentaries). Instagram entails all these elements in one app. It can also circulate pictures and videos instantly and across multiple platforms. Third, since the tool relies on visual presentations it is likely to trigger students' creativity and sharpen their aesthetics when they share photos, videos and stories. Nevertheless, Instagram has a flip side. It is designed for entertainment rather than for language learning. Additionally, some Instagram content is not school-appropriate since Instagram is about the digital advertising of luxury products. When Instagram is used for L2 learning, teachers need to think out of the box when designing e-Portfolio-based lessons.

Instagram probably has high to moderate practicality depending on the extent to which teachers integrate the tool in their e-Portfolio curriculum. Although Instagram has recently introduced video-sharing features, its video-editing technique is far from satisfactory. After all, Instagram remains an image-based digital tool. For classroom instruction, teachers may create a public account and invite students to contribute posts and collaborate with one another by using that account to protect their privacy. They can also ask students to create posts based upon one language skill, namely writing. For instance, students can search related videos on the internet, compose an Instagram story to narrate how they improved their writing during home-based learning and share these stories on the feed for peer comments. In visual arts classes, teachers can encourage students to upload their art pieces (hand-drawn or computer-generated imagery) on Instagram and utilise the tool as a browsable gallery for appreciation.

Summary

Chapter 8 introduced four categories of e-Portfolio tools that have been widely adopted at the classroom level, including self-authoring tools, Web 2.0 applications, commercial e-Portfolio software and social media platforms. These common tools were then evaluated by means of multimodality, mobility, instantaneous participation and interactivity. The chapter went on to discuss emerging issues arising from the implementation of these digital tools, such as reflection, evidence, multimedia components and multiple presentations. It then reviewed six tools that can be utilised as e-Portfolio platforms: Google Classroom, Microsoft Teams, Schoology, Nearpod, Anthology Portfolio and Instagram.

9 Future Directions for e-Portfolios

Introduction

Chapter 9 first recapitulates the whole book by providing a synopsis of each chapter. It then unpacks major takeaways when readers use the book in specific applied linguistics or language teacher education programmes. Afterwards, the chapter discusses three future directions for e-Portfolio pedagogy and research in L2 contexts. To conclude, the section titled 'Resources' offers readers additional information if they plan to apply e-Portfolios at work or for study.

Synopsis of the Book

The book starts with a prelude by introducing what paper-based and electronic portfolios are and how they are implemented in first language (L1) and second language (L2) educational environments. This prologue provides definitions of key concepts for the book and describes the current assessment landscape to contextualise e-Portfolio integration. Chapter 1 introduces the origin of paper-based portfolios and their transition to an electronic medium near the turn of the century. It presents various types and mediums of e-Portfolios and their pros and cons. The role of e-Portfolios in language education and L2 writing classrooms is then discussed.

Chapter 2 reviews the e-Portfolio literature by identifying its research into three elements, namely product, process and tool, and then by categorising related studies in terms of teaching, learning and assessment at various educational levels in L2 contexts. Chapter 3 unpacks the theoretical underpinnings of e-Portfolios and e-Portfolio assessment. It first introduces the elements, attributes and processes of e-Portfolios and then discusses three theories underlying e-Portfolios: socio-constructivism, assessment for learning and metacognition. Definitions, conceptual debates, applications and integration challenges are further addressed in accordance with each theory. Teacher beliefs and practices about e-Portfolio integration are discussed.

Chapter 4 presents the features and elements of e-Portfolio curricula followed by an illustration of how four language skills are taught within an e-Portfolio programme. Three approaches to e-Portfolio integration into English curricula are introduced: the blended, provisional and personal approach. A four-step model on designing e-Portfolio curricula is included. Chapter 5 is about e-Portfolio assessment. It delineates two broad assessment paradigms and reveals two common assessment purposes plus their relationship. The chapter further discusses the advantages and limitations of e-Portfolio assessment. It proposes practical strategies concerning how teachers can align instruction, learning and assessment via e-Portfolios.

Chapter 6 investigates 34 adolescent students' perspectives of e-Portfolio compilation, their conceptions of e-Portfolio assessment and their emotion experience. Qualitative findings are reported after an analysis of an online survey, semi-structured interviews and e-Portfolio artefacts. The informants were mostly positive about their e-Portfolio compilation journeys despite some issues such as privacy and fairness. Chapter 7 examines how two English language teachers transitioned from in-person to remote teaching, and the extent to which they integrated e-Portfolios into their instruction during the pandemic. This qualitative study underscored the teachers' technology integration, its affordances and constraints. Three post-pandemic lessons learnt from this case study are discussed to make e-Portfolio integration sustainable.

Chapter 8 presents a commentary on e-Portfolio tools. It first describes four types of e-Portfolios and then evaluates e-Portfolio applications by way of four aspects of technological innovation. The second half of the chapter reviews six up-to-date digital software, which can be used as e-Portfolio tools. To conclude, the current chapter summarises the contents of the book. It offers prospective readers major takeaways if they plan to integrate the e-Portfolio method into their L2 instruction. Future directions for adopting e-Portfolios in L2 teaching and assessment in a wider educational landscape are suggested.

Key Takeaways

While e-Portfolios and e-Portfolio assessment are not new in language education, this book provides teachers, educators, undergraduate/postgraduate students, applied linguists and scholars with an informed perspective and a rich catalogue of evidence-based as well as actionable ideas when they plan to initiate and research into this alternative teaching-cum-assessment method. To summarise, target readers are likely to benefit from the following three takeaways.

E-Portfolios as an instructional method

Because of their flexibility, accessibility and transparency, e-Portfolios can be used as a viable instructional method after the pandemic.

E-Portfolios can enhance teachers' digital literacy by upgrading their L2 instructional approaches when they adopt various types and mediums of e-Portfolios (cf. Chapter 1). E-Portfolios are a perfect fit for (emergency) remote teaching, especially these days when most learning management systems are easy to use. Even after face-to-face classes resume, teachers may allocate part of their instructional hours to e-Portfolio pedagogy, since this online programme does not affect daily curriculum delivery (cf. Chapter 4). Concerning technology integration, e-Portfolios can be duly incorporated into existing English curricula in accordance with teacher beliefs, institutional demands and students' learning needs (cf. Chapters 4 and 7). As there are numerous digital application tools on the market, teachers may make an informed decision to select a user-friendly one, appropriate for their teaching styles and classroom agendas (cf. Chapter 8 and Resources).

E-Portfolios as a learning-orientated software application

While schools adopt e-Portfolios as a learning management system, students can make full use of this platform to create, compile and reflect upon their artefacts. After all, students' active participation in creating, curating, reflecting and disseminating portfolio work may enhance motivation, self-efficacy, independence and metacognition in L2 learning (cf. Chapters 1 and 2). In addition to on-campus applications, students can use e-Portfolio platforms to support their out-of-school learning as a digital companion and develop their legitimate L2 learner identity over time (cf. Chapter 6). By so doing, students can foster a sense of ownership and achievement while compiling their e-Portfolios. Although teachers may restrict students to upload certain genres and modalities of artefacts as part of the coursework, students should think out of the box by uploading graphic, audio, video or virtual reality-based assignments to showcase their L2 learning formatively (cf. Chapter 8). The creation of multimedia artefacts can broaden students' L2 learning strategies and facilitate their computer literacy.

E-Portfolios as an alternative assessment

Apart from language teaching, e-Portfolios can be used as an assessment method, especially when face-to-face instruction is suspended (cf. Chapters 1 and 6). Using e-Portfolios to serve their formative purpose, teachers can promote self and peer assessments, self-reflection, collaborative writing and project work (cf. Chapter 3). Using e-Portfolios to serve their summative purpose, teachers may decide what artefacts and genres they will evaluate, which phase of e-Portfolio compilation they will assess and whether or not they assign students an 'individual' or a 'group' grade owing to its collective nature (cf. Chapter 5). With these dual assessment purposes in mind, e-Portfolios would be a better alternative to conventional paper-and-pencil assessments because they provide a wider spectrum of what students can and cannot do throughout their e-Portfolio development journeys among teachers, parents, principals and the students themselves (cf. Chapter 6). In addition, teachers can interpret related e-Portfolio assessment data to inform and modify their L2 instruction accordingly. Through e-feedback provided to students on e-Portfolios, teachers can implement assessment *for* learning promptly and effectively.

Future Directions

To further explore the classroom applications of e-Portfolios and research into their effectiveness for L2 learning, there are three future directions for educators' and researchers' consideration.

Language assessment literacy in e-Portfolios

There has been a large body of research into language assessment literacy, yet little attention has been paid to understanding how to enhance teachers' and students' e-Portfolio assessment literacy in order to facilitate their active engagement in portfolio pedagogy and compilation experiences, respectively (Lam, 2022b). Although most studies examine the short-term effects of e-Portfolio programmes on learners' acquisition of L2 skills, namely speaking and writing, there has been an apparent lack of longitudinal research exploring learners' development of their language assessment literacy trajectories within school-based e-Portfolio programmes, particularly at the K-12 levels (Gan & Lam, 2022; Tsagari, 2021). L2 assessment scholars can target these two emerging research agendas to develop a better understanding of what (components), why (theoretical rationale) and how (behavioural acts) to enhance teacher and student assessment literacy and facilitate the usefulness of e-Portfolio assessment in authentic classroom contexts (Yancey, 2019). Likewise, teachers need to cultivate their computer literacy by attending regular professional development training in e-learning and/or e-assessment via webinars or regional/international conferences. After doing so, they can provide customised training to their students. As Yancey (2009) has claimed, e-Portfolios can be successfully implemented if both teachers and students are computer literate.

Emotional aspect of e-Portfolio compilation

As revealed in Chapter 6, the emotional aspect of L2 learning via an e-Portfolio remains underrepresented because adolescent students tend to engage in e-Portfolio tasks better if they have higher self-efficacy beliefs than their counterparts (Zheng & Barrot, 2022). Existing scholarship has mainly emphasised the cognitive, motivational and linguistic aspects of e-Portfolio assessment by identifying whether e-Portfolio interventions can improve student L2 learning. However, little has been done to understand how the impact of e-Portfolio applications may influence students' emotional well-being when students are learning an L2 during and beyond the pandemic (Lam *et al.*, 2023). While students may have diverse affective reactions to e-Portfolios, their emotional experiences play a crucial part in the e-Portfolio process, which possibly need moral support, encouragement and positive reinforcement from peers and teachers if they want to sustain e-Portfolio learning (Crisol Moya *et al.*, 2021). In future, mixed methods should be adopted to examine learners' emotional attachment to e-Portfolio assessment (e.g. contribution, responsibility, investment or self-motivation). Quantitatively, tried-and-tested scales can be adapted or replicated to measure learner change in emotions. Qualitatively, narrative enquiry using narrative frames could yield insightful and contextualised data to understand students' emotional experiences of e-Portfolio compilation.

Use of social media as e-Portfolio platforms

In practice and research, teachers and scholars have adopted intranets, weblogs and learning management systems or have customised e-Portfolio software tools as e-Portfolio platforms (Farrell, 2020). Notwithstanding the availability and accessibility of these tools, educators and researchers have started to identify other alternatives to host student e-Portfolios for teaching and research. One prominent example is Facebook. The rise of using social media as e-Portfolio tools is threefold. First, most social media apps can be downloaded and browsed using various digital gadgets, such as mobiles, laptops, desktops and tablets as long as there is a wifi connection. Second, students always use social media to communicate with peers, friends, acquaintances and parents, every day and everywhere. Third, most social media platforms permit creating, sharing and publishing information via multimedia artefacts, particularly image-based sites (i.e. Instagram), to enhance high connectivity with others. Currently, studies are investigating how Facebook-based and Instagram-based e-Portfolio sites enhance students' development of writing and speaking skills in course-based settings (e.g. Lee, 2022; Zheng & Barrot, 2022). Despite these pioneering studies, more has to be done to explore how other popular social media platforms could be used to support L2 students' language learning in virtual environments, including YouTube, WhatsApp and TikTok.

Summary

Chapter 9 summarised the content of each chapter. It subsequently discussed three takeaways after prospective readers finished this monograph. For instance, how e-Portfolios could be used as a pedagogical approach to facilitate flipped teaching, a learning-orientated software tool to facilitate self- and co-regulation of language learning and an alternative assessment method to promote the fairness and inclusiveness of L2 assessment during the post-pandemic era. Then, three future directions for e-Portfolio classroom applications and research were recommended, including enhancing stakeholder language assessment literacy, exploring the emotional aspect of e-Portfolio compilation and utilising social media sites as e-Portfolio platforms. To enhance readers' conceptual understanding and classroom practices, an additional section titled 'Resources' is presented after Chapter 9.

Appendix A: Questionnaire

Part 1: Basic Information 基本資料

Name 姓名:

Age 年齡:

Gender 性別:

Grade 年級:

Class 班別:

Part 2: Previous Experiences 過往經歷

Please share with us your previous experiences. 請根據你的實際經歷回答下列問題。

(1) Do you use a digital device (e.g. computers, smart phones or tablets) frequently?
你是否經常使用電子設備（如電腦，智能手機或平板電腦）?

- Yes, every day. 是，每天使用。

- Yes, several days a week, but not every day. 是，每週會使用幾天，但不是每天都用。

- No, a few hours a week. 不是，每週僅使用幾小時。

- No, seldom. 不是，幾乎不用。

(2) Did you have any experience of creating an e-Portfolio before this course? 此前你是否使用過電子檔案?

(3) Before this course, have you published on any of the following internet sources? 你此前是否在以下渠道發布過內容?

- Personal websites or blogs 個人網站或博客.

- Photo websites (e.g. Facebook, Instagram) 圖片網站（如臉書，IG).

- Video websites (e.g. YouTube, TikTok) 視頻網站（如YouTube, 抖音).

- Podcasts 播客.

- None of the above 以上均沒有.

(4) I am confident to use the following applications: 我能夠熟練運用以下應用程序：

- Messaging apps (e.g. WhatsApp, Line, WeChat, email)
  信息類應用（如WhatsApp，Line，微信，電子郵件）.
- Online shopping apps (e.g. Amazon, Taobao) 在線購物類應用（如亞馬遜，淘寶）.
- Streaming apps (e.g. Netflix, Disney+) 視頻播放類應用 （如奈飛，迪士尼+）.
- Online video game apps 網絡遊戲類應用.
- Academic apps (e.g. Grammarly, dictionary) 學術類應用 (如Grammarly，詞典).
- None of the above 以上均沒有.

(5) Please tick if you have the following computer skill(s) 請勾選你擁有的技能：

- Information search 信息搜索.
- Word processing 文字處理.
- Graphical design 圖形設計.
- Presentation software 演示軟件.
- HTML 網頁語言.
- Video editing 視頻編輯.
- Audio editing 音頻編輯.
- Digital photography 電子攝影.
- None of the above 以上均沒有.

Note: Items in Parts 3–5 are designed for a Likert scale of 5, with '1' denoting strongly disagree and '5' denoting strongly agree.

Part 3: E-Portfolio Compilation 檔案彙編

There are 12 questions in Part 3. In this part, we would like to know how you create, compile and manage your e-Portfolio. 第三部分包含12項題目。我們想瞭解你如何創建、編寫和管理自己的電子檔案。

(1) E-Portfolio expectations were clearly stated in this course.
課程中清晰地描述了理想的電子檔案是什麼樣子。

(2) E-Portfolio procedures were clearly stated in this course.
課程中清晰地描述了編寫電子檔案的過程。

(3) I could create artefacts in my e-Portfolio independently. 我能獨立在電子檔案中創建作品。

(4) I could compile and manage the e-Portfolio content proficiently.
我能熟練編寫和管理電子檔案的內容。

(5) I often talked about e-Portfolio requirements with my classmates.
我經常與同學討論電子檔案。

(6) I would use an e-Portfolio to showcase my work to my friends.
我會用電子檔案向朋友們展示自己的學習成果。

(7) I would use an e-Portfolio to showcase my work to my family.
我會用電子檔案向家人展示自己的學習成果。

(8) I consider teacher feedback on my e-Portfolio as constructive criticism.
我把老師對電子檔案的評語作為建設性意見。

(9) I learn from my mistakes through e-Portfolio compilation.
編寫電子檔案幫助我從錯誤中學習。

(10) I plan to visit the e-Portfolios of others in the future. 我計劃將來查看其他人的電子檔案。

(11) I will update my e-Portfolio in the future even if it does not become a course requirement. 即使課程沒有要求，我將來也會更新我的電子檔案。

(12) I plan to continue to upgrade my e-Portfolio for lifelong learning. 我打算持續改進我的電子檔案以作終生學習之用。

Part 4: Conceptions of Assessment 評估觀念

There are 16 questions in Part 4. In this part, we would like to know your conceptions of e-Portfolio assessment in terms of purpose, creation, learning goal, artefact, reflection and attitude. 第四部分包含16項題目。我們想從目的、創建、學習目標、作品、反思和態度等方面，瞭解你對電子檔案評估的看法。

(1) My purpose for using an e-Portfolio is to improve my academic performance. 我使用電子檔案是爲了提升學業表現。(purpose)

(2) My purpose for using an e-Portfolio is to monitor my skills (e.g. word processing) and knowledge (e.g. English grammar) development. 我將電子檔案作爲一種記錄自己技能提升（如處理文字）和知識積纍（如英文語法）的方式。(purpose)

(3) Using an e-Portfolio in this course assists the teacher to better assess my knowledge. 在本課程中使用電子檔案讓老師能更好地評估我的知識。(purpose)

(4) I use my e-Portfolio to reach my learning goals, such as developing my skills (e.g. word processing) and knowledge. 我用電子檔案達成學習目標，例如培養技能（如處理文字）和積纍知識（如英文語法）。(learning goal)

(5) My e-Portfolio helped me fulfil my learning goal continuously. 電子檔案幫助我不斷達成各個階段的學習目標。(learning goal)

(6) I have the opportunity to create different types of multimedia artefacts (e.g. video clips, audio and photos) in my e-Portfolio. 我有機會在自己的電子檔案中添加各種多媒體作品（如視頻，音頻或照片）。(artefact)

(7) I have fun creating multimedia artefacts in my e-Portfolio. 製作多媒體電子檔案給我帶來了樂趣。(artefact)

(8) My e-Portfolio assisted me to reflect on my goals and accomplishments. 電子檔案有助於我反思學習目標和成果。(reflection)

(9) The use of e-Portfolios helped me in understanding and reflecting on my learning progress. 使用電子檔案能幫助我反思自己的學習進程。(reflection)

(10) Reading the e-Portfolios of others enriched my understanding and reflection on the learning process. 閱讀其他人的電子檔案幫助我更好地理解和反思學習過程。(reflection)

(11) To create and maintain an e-Portfolio in the course was easier than I expected. 使用電子檔案比我預想得更容易。(creation)

(12) The process of creating my e-Portfolio was not time-consuming. 創建電子檔案的過程並沒有花費我太多時間。(creation)

(13) The use of e-Portfolios enhanced my study attitude to learn. 使用電子檔案培養了我良好的學習態度。(attitude)

(14) I benefited from browsing my classmates' e-Portfolios. 閱讀同學們的電子檔案讓我受益。(attitude)

(15) Browsing my classmates' e-Portfolios would be a valuable learning experience. 閱讀同學們的電子檔案是一種寶貴的學習經歷。(attitude)

(16) My attitude towards an e-Portfolio is positive because it is a better way for teachers to assess my knowledge than a multiple-choice or essay test. 我對電子檔案持積極態度，因爲與多選測驗題或作文考試相比，電子檔案是更好的知識評估方式。(attitude)

Part 5: Emotional Experiences 情感體驗

There are 17 questions in Part 5. In this part, please share your emotional experiences when you engage in the e-Portfolio assessment process, and how your emotional experiences are mediated by individual, institutional and contextual factors. 第5部分包含17項題目。請分享你在電子檔案評估過程中的情感體驗，以及個人、學校和環境因素如何影響你的情感體驗。

(1)	I like the layout of my e-Portfolio. 我喜歡電子檔案的佈局。
(2)	I like creating my e-Portfolio. 我喜歡編寫電子檔案。
(3)	I feel easy using my e-Portfolio with good access to the internet. 如果有穩定快速的網絡，我覺得電子檔案就會更容易使用。
(4)	I value the integration of e-Portfolios in the course. 我認為在課程中融入電子檔案十分有價值。
(5)	My e-Portfolio helps me to communicate better with my classmates. 電子檔案幫助我更好地與同學交流。
(6)	My e-Portfolio helps me to communicate more effectively with my teacher. 電子檔案幫助我更有效地與老師溝通。
(7)	Compared to other courses without e-Portfolio use, I feel more connected with students in this course. 與不采用電子檔案的課程相比，我覺得自己與本課程中的同學聯係更緊密。
(8)	I like sharing my e-Portfolio with my classmates. 我喜歡與同學們分享我的電子檔案。
(9)	I am more willing to ask questions and share comments after I read my classmates' e-Portfolios. 閱讀了同學的電子檔案之後，我提出問題和分享觀點的意願更強烈了。
(10)	My teacher gets to know me better than teachers in other courses because I shared my e-Portfolio with him/her. 本課的老師比其它課的老師更瞭解我，因為我跟他/她分享了我的電子檔案。
(11)	Because we share our e-Portfolios, I feel an increased level of trust towards my classmates in the course. 因為分享了彼此的電子檔案，我感覺更加信任此課程中的同學。
(12)	Sharing my e-Portfolio with other classmates helps me feel like I am part of a community. 與同學分享我的電子檔案讓我感覺自己是集體中的一員。
(13)	I feel comfortable with an e-Portfolio to be graded by teachers in a course. 我不介意老師在課程中對我的電子檔案進行評分。
(14)	I feel comfortable with an e-Portfolio to be part of the non-graded assignment in a course. 我不介意把電子檔案作為課程中不評分作業的一部分。
(15)	I hope the confidentiality of my e-Portfolio can be ensured. 我希望我的電子檔案可以確保良好的私密性。
(16)	I hope my e-Portfolio will be 'useful work' – instead of a sheer collection of 'electronic worksheets'. 我希望自己的電子檔案可以"學以致用" —— 而不是一堆"電子功課紙"。
(17)	I hope assessment of my e-Portfolio could be objective and without errors in judgement. 我希望對電子檔案的評估能保持客觀，不會出現誤判。

Part 6: Open-Ended Questions 開放式問題

There are 4 questions in Part 6. Please give your answers in either *English* or *Chinese*. 第6部分包4項題目。請使用英文或中文作答。

(1) What is your understanding of an e-Portfolio? What is it used for? How did you use it? 你認爲電子檔案是什麼？它有什麼用途？你又是如何使用它的？ (conceptions)

(2) Did you get support(s) when you were creating your e-Portfolio (e.g. extra reading materials, conference with teachers, relevant hyperlinks)? If any, please describe one episode when you got support. 在使用電子檔案的過程中，你是否獲得了幫助和支持？如有，請擇一場景舉例說明。

(3) What benefit(s) and drawback(s) did you experience while keeping your e-Portfolio in the course? 在本課程中使用電子檔案，給你帶來了什麼益處或不便？ (compilations)

(4) Do you like or dislike using an e-Portfolio? Please state the reason(s). 你喜歡/不喜歡電子檔案嗎？請詳述原因。 (emotions)

Appendix B: Interview Guide for Adolescent Students

(1) What is the theme of your e-Portfolio?
(2) Can you briefly describe how you create and compile your e-Portfolio?
(3) Which aspect(s) do you like most about your e-Portfolio?
(4) What are the most enjoyable moments throughout your portfolio compilation?
(5) What are the most challenging moments throughout your portfolio compilation?
(6) What are your emotions when you observe growth, efforts or achievements in your e-Portfolio? Do you have any particular thoughts you want to share with me?
(7) How do you think about your contributions to the e-Portfolio works? Do you have a sense of achievement, a sense of belonging or a sense of satisfaction?
(8) Finally, tell me what difficulties you have come across when you engage in various portfolio activities, namely your personal beliefs, motivation, time constraint, support from teachers, etc.

Resources

A. Digital Tools as e-Portfolio Platforms

(1) Google Classroom (https://edu.google.com/workspace-for-education/classroom/)

Choose the edition that's right for your institution

Use flexible, secure tools at no cost with Education Fundamentals, or add the enhanced capabilities you need with Education Standard, the Teaching and Learning Upgrade, or Education Plus.

Every edition includes

Gmail Calendar Meet Docs Sheets Slides Forms Classroom Assignments Sites Groups Drive Admin Tasks Jamboard

- A free and flexible application that is suitable for all education levels.
- It can be used together with many other Google apps, such as Gmail, Docs and Jamboard, to meet the different requirements of teachers.

(2) **Microsoft Teams (https://www.microsoft.com/en-us/education/ products/teams)**

- A powerful product for teachers to manage their classrooms and build an e-portfolio with their students on PCs, tablets and mobiles.
- More suitable for secondary-level school students or above and requires subscription.
- Students need to be tech-savvy to switch among various functions.

(3) **Mahara (https://mahara.org/)**

- A customised e-Portfolio application for students to build academic e-Portfolios and engage with their supervisors and teammates.
- Free and open-source, more suitable for post-secondary students or above.

(4) **Flip (https://info.flip.com/)**

Share a topic and discuss, whenever you like

Post a topic to your group to begin learning and sharing together!

- Host book clubs with anyone around the world
- Build more personal connections with remote employees
- Learn a new language with video coaching and feedback

- An app that supports teachers to create video-based instructional materials on an e-Portfolio platform that enhances more discussion and communication with students.
- Suitable for all education levels, and free of charge.

(5) **Seesaw (https://web.seesaw.me/)**

Great Instruction Happens on Seesaw

CLASSROOM TECH SIMPLIFIED	AGENCY & CREATION STARTING IN PRE-K	SEE WHAT STUDENTS *ACTUALLY* KNOW	KEEP EVERYONE IN THE LEARNING LOOP
Flexible instructional tools build upon what you're already doing for a balanced approach	Intuitive learning tools empower student voice, critical thinking, and ownership in all grades	Digital portfolios make thinking visible and share growth with an authentic audience	Inclusive communication tools engage teachers, admin, and families around learning

- A popular e-Portfolio site and interactive learning management system where teachers can create authentic multimedia experiences for PreK-12 students.

(6) Bulb (https://my.bulbapp.com/)

bulb is your place to shine™

With a powerful portfolio + resume in one, bulb allows professionals, educators, and students to put their best foot forward in school, career, and life.

Users can easily and beautifully demonstrate growth, contextualize skills, and use their unique voice to show the world who they truly are.

- Bulb is a website that assists learners to create and publish digital portfolios, with a flexible and attractive interface for students of all education levels.
- Teachers can get a free upgrade to Bulb+ which includes unlimited portfolio pages and storage space.

(7) ClassDojo (https://www.classdojo.com/)

ClassDojo   Plus   About us   Schools   Resources   Log in   Sign up

Flourishing classroom communities, flourishing kids

Loved by more than 50 million students and parents.
Free for teachers, forever.

Get started as a...

Teacher   Parent   Student   School Leader

- With a focus on communication, ClassDojo is an online classroom management system and app where teachers can track student classroom behaviours and learning progress by creating an e-Portfolio for each student.
- The platform is designed for K-6 students, and free for teachers.

(8) Facebook (https://www.facebook.com/)

- A popular social networking site to connect students, friends, teachers and parents. Students can build their e-Portfolios by posting pictures, texts, audios and/or videos to their accounts.
- The tool is free of charge; however, only students aged 13+ are eligible for registration.

B. International Journals that Publish e-Portfolio Studies

(1) *Computer Assisted Language Learning* (https://www.tandfonline.com/toc/ncal20/current)
   Annual subscription required; Print ISSN: 0958-8221 and Online ISSN: 1744-3210; eight issues per year.
(2) *Computers and Education* (https://www.sciencedirect.com/journal/computers-and-education)
   Annual subscription required; ISSN: 0360-1315; 12 issues per year.
(3) *International Journal of e-Portfolios* (https://www.theijep.com/)
   Open-access; ISSN 2157-622X; two issues per year.
(4) *The Internet and Higher Education* (https://www.sciencedirect.com/journal/the-internet-and-higher-education)
   Annual subscription required; ISSN 1096-7516; four issues per year.

C. Recently Published Journal Articles on e-Portfolios

Barrot, J.S. (2020) Effects of Facebook-based e-Portfolio on ESL learners' writing performance. *Language, Culture and Curriculum* 34 (1), 95–111. https://doi.org/10.1080/07908318.2020.1745822

Fathi, J. and Rahimi, M. (2022) Electronic writing portfolio in a collaborative writing environment: Its impact on EFL students' writing performance. *Computer Assisted Language Learning*, 1–39. https://doi.org/10.1080/09588221.2022.2097697

Khodi, A., Khezerlou, H. and Sahraei, H. (2022) Dependability and utility of using e-Portfolios in assessing EFL learners' speaking proficiency. *Computer Assisted Language Learning*, 1–23. https://doi.org/10.1080/09588221.2022.2093379

Lam, R. (2022) E-portfolios for self-regulated and co-regulated learning: A review. *Frontiers in Psychology* 13, 1079385. https://doi.org/10.3389/fpsyg.2022.1079385

Lam, R. (2023) E-portfolios: What we know, what we don't, and what we need to know. *RELC Journal* 54 (1), 208–215. https://doi.org/10.1177/0033688220974102

Osawa, K. (2023) Integrating automated written corrective feedback into e-Portfolios for second language writing: Notion and Notion AI. *RELC Journal*. https://doi.org/10.1177/00336882231198913

Pourdana, N. and Tavassoli, K. (2022) Differential impacts of e-Portfolio assessment on language learners' engagement modes and genre-based writing improvement. *Language Testing in Asia* 12 (1). https://doi.org/10.1186/s40468-022-00156-7

Zheng, Y. and Barrot, J.S. (2022) Social media as an e-Portfolio platform: Effects on L2 learners' speaking performance. *Language Learning & Technology* 26 (1), 1–19.

D. Websites on e-Portfolio Examples

(1) **Australian e-Portfolio Project** by the Australian Federal Government Office of Learning and Teaching https://research.qut.edu.au/eportfolio/
(2) **EU Classroom e-Portfolios Project (EUfolio)** by the European Commission http://eufolio.eu/
(3) **The e-Assessment (eAA)** by Cambridge Assessment https://www.e-assessment.com/resources/e-portfolios/
(4) **Online Portfolio** by the Council of Europe https://www.coe.int/en/web/youth-portfolio/online-portfolio

E. Monographs about e-Portfolios

(1) Chaudhuri, T. and Cabau, B. (eds) (2018) *E-portfolios in Higher Education: A Multidisciplinary Approach*. Springer.

- This book is a collection of articles on e-Portfolio usage in various subject discipline courses. It gives an overview of e-Portfolio development within the context of higher education.
  Link on HKBU Library
(2) Eynon, B. and Gambino, L.M. (2017) *High-Impact e-Portfolio Practice: A Catalyst for Student, Faculty, and Institutional Learning.* Stylus Publishing, LLC.
  - Targeting higher education, this book unpacks e-Portfolio applications with a catalyst framework, principles and strategies. It primarily focuses on the use of e-Portfolios at an advanced level, although it also provides case scenarios and guidelines to help teachers design context-specific e-Portfolio curricula in courses and programmes.
  Link on Google Books
(3) Lam, R. and Moorhouse, B.L. (2022) *Using Digital Portfolios to Develop Students' Writing: A Practical Guide for Language Teachers.* Routledge.
  - Targeting primary- and secondary-level language teachers, this book provides an easy-to-read guide to set up digital portfolios in classrooms by introducing theories in the first half of the book and then applying them in three vignettes.
  Link on Publisher Site
(4) Renwick, M. (2017) *Digital Portfolios in the Classroom: Showcasing and Assessing Student Work.* ASCD.
  - Starting with the definition of digital portfolios, the author goes on by narrating how to make a case and get started with digital portfolios with students in class and schoolwide in a comprehensive way.
  Link on HKBU Library
(5) Reynolds, C. and Patton, J. (2014) *Leveraging the ePortfolio for Integrative Learning: A Faculty Guide to Classroom Practices for Transforming Student Learning.* Stylus Publishing, LLC.
  - This book is written for instructors who plan to integrate university student learning via e-Portfolios. First, the authors introduce the ideas of e-Portfolios and integrative learning, followed by their relationship. Second, the authors discuss how to combine the two concepts in pedagogy and curriculum design. Third, they demonstrate how instructors can use e-Portfolios to assess student learning with rubrics.
  Link on Google Books
(6) Yancey, K.B. (ed.) (2019) *ePortfolio as Curriculum: Models and Practices for Developing Students' ePortfolio Literacy.* Stylus Publishing, LLC.

- By analysing case studies in different US universities, this book penetrates a set of frameworks and models useful for guiding students in designing and creating e-Portfolios.

Link on Google Books

F. YouTube Tutorials on Setting Up e-Portfolios

(1) **Google Classroom** – Getting Started with Google Classroom | EDTech Made Easy – GOOGLE CLASSROOM TUTORIAL

https://www.youtube.com/watch?v=rCNImsWUxZA&t=15s
- A hands-on tutorial for teachers who want to integrate an e-Portfolio in their class from scratch. This video introduces key functions that teachers need to know when they get started on the platform.

(2) **Microsoft Teams** – How to Teach Online with Microsoft Teams – A Guide for Teachers

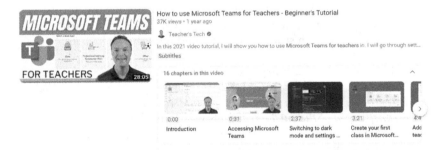

https://www.youtube.com/watch?v=5-2t-KSPlqE
- This video clip goes through the steps of registration, adding students, communicating with students and giving assignments to them on Microsoft Teams.

(3) **Seesaw** – The Seesaw Tutorial for Teachers – Updated 2022

https://www.youtube.com/watch?v=auUgZHsXY-0

- A straightforward tutorial that introduces how to set up the Seesaw classroom in a step-by-step way, starting from registration, account and class setting, and then activity creation.

References

Abrar-ul-Hassan, S., Douglas, D. and Turner, J. (2021) Revisiting second language portfolio assessment in a new age. *System* 103, 102652.

Acker, S.R. and Halasek, K. (2008) Preparing high school students for college-level writing: Using ePortfolio to support a successful transition. *The Journal of General Education* 57 (1), 1–14.

Al Kahtani, S. (1999) Electronic portfolios in ESL writing: An alternative approach. *Computer Assisted Language Learning* 12 (3), 261–268.

Allal, L. (2020) Assessment and the co-regulation of learning in the classroom. *Assessment in Education: Principles, Policy & Practice* 27 (4), 332–349.

Allal, L. (2021) Involving primary school students in the co-construction of formative assessment in support of writing. *Assessment in Education: Principles, Policy & Practice* 28 (5–6), 584–601.

Alonso, F., López, G., Manrique, D. and Viñes, J.M. (2005) An instructional model for web-based e-learning education with a blended learning process approach. *British Journal of Educational Technology* 36 (2), 217–235.

Al-Qallaf, C.L. and Al-Mutairi, A.S.R. (2016) Digital literacy and digital content supports learning: The impact of blogs on teaching English as a foreign language. *The Electronic Library* 34 (3), 522–547.

Alvarez, A. and Moxley, D. (2004) The student portfolio in social work education. *Journal of Teaching and Social Work* 24 (1/2), 87–103.

Andrade, H.L. (2019) A critical review of research on student self-assessment. *Frontiers in Education* 4 (87). https://doi.org/3389/feduc.2019.00087

Assessment Reform Group (2002) Assessment for learning. https://www.hkeaa.edu.hk/doclibrary/sba/hkdse/eng_dvd/doc/Afl_principles.pdf

Aydin, S. (2014) EFL writers' attitudes and perceptions towards F-portfolio use. *TechTrends* 58 (2), 59–77.

Aygün, S. and Aydin, S. (2016) The use of e-Portfolio in EFL writing: A review of literature. *ELT Research Journal* 5 (3), 205–217.

Bader, M., Burner, T., Iversen, S.H. and Varga, Z. (2019) Student perspectives on formative feedback as part of writing portfolios. *Assessment & Evaluation in Higher Education* 44 (7), 1017–1028.

Baeten, M., Dochy, F. and Struyven, K. (2008) Students' approaches to learning and assessment preferences in a portfolio-based learning environment. *Instructional Science* 36 (5), 359–374.

Bakla, A. (2020) A mixed methods study of feedback modes in L2 writing. *Language Learning & Technology* 24 (1), 107–128.

Barrett, H.C. (2007) Researching electronic portfolios and learner engagement: The REFLECT Initiative. *Journal of Adolescent & Adult Literacy* 50 (6), 436–449.

Barrett, H.C. (2010) Balancing the two faces of e-Portfolios. *Educação, Formação & Tecnologias* 3 (1), 6–14.

Barrot, J.S. (2016) Using Facebook-based e-portfolio in ESL writing classrooms: Impact and challenges. *Language, Culture, and Curriculum* 29 (3), 286–301.

Barrot, J.S. (2021) Effects of Facebook-based e-Portfolio on ESL learners' writing performance. *Language, Culture and Curriculum* 34 (1), 95–111.

Baturay, M.H. and Daloğlu, A. (2010) E-Portfolio assessment in an online English language course. *Computer Assisted Language Learning* 23 (5), 413–428.

Becker, C. (2015) Assessment and portfolios. In J. Bland (ed.) *Teaching English to Young Learners: Critical Issues in Language Teaching with 3–12 Year Olds* (pp. 261–278). Bloomsbury.

Beckers, J., Dolmans, D. and van Merriënboer, J. (2016) ePortfolios enhancing students' self-directed learning: A systematic review of influencing factors. *Australasian Journal of Educational Technology* 32 (2), 32–46.

Belanoff, P. and Dickson, M. (eds) (1991) *Portfolios: Process and Product.* Boynton/Cook Heineman.

Belgrad, S.F. (2013) Portfolios and e-Portfolios: Student reflection, self-assessment, and goal-setting in the learning process. In J.H. McMillan (ed.) *Sage Handbook of Research on Classroom Assessment* (pp. 331–346). Sage.

Bennett, R.E. (2011) Formative assessment: A critical review. *Assessment in Education: Principles, Policy & Practice* 18 (1), 5–25.

Black, P. (2015) Formative assessment – An optimistic but incomplete vision. *Assessment in Education: Principles, Policy & Practice* 22 (1), 161–177.

Black, P. and Wiliam, D. (2009) Developing the theory of formative assessment. *Educational Assessment, Evaluation and Accountability* 21 (1), 5–31.

Black, P. and Wiliam, D. (2018) Classroom assessment and pedagogy. *Assessment in Education: Principles, Policy & Practice* 25 (6), 551–575.

Bolliger, D.U. and Shepherd, C.E. (2010) Student perceptions of e-Portfolio integration in online courses. *Distance Education* 31 (3), 295–314.

Bowman, J., Lowe, B.J., Sabourin, K. and Sweet, C.S. (2016) The use of ePortfolios to support metacognitive practice in a first-year writing program. *International Journal of ePortfolio* 6 (1), 1–22.

Bozkurt, G. (2017) Social constructivism: Does it succeed in reconciling individual cognition with social teaching and learning practices in mathematics? *Journal of Education and Practice* 8 (3), 210–218.

Bryant, L.H. and Chittum, J.R. (2013) ePortfolio effectiveness: A(n ill-fated) search for empirical support. *International Journal of ePortfolio* 3 (2), 189–198.

Burner, T. (2014) The potential formative benefits of portfolio assessment in second and foreign language writing contexts: A review of the literature. *Studies in Educational Evaluation* 43, 139–149.

Burns, A. and Siegel, J. (2018) Teaching the four language skills: Themes and issues. In A. Burns and J. Siegel (eds) *International Perspectives on Teaching the Four Skills in ELT: Listening, Speaking, Reading, Writing* (pp. 1–17). Palgrave MacMillan.

Burns, E.B. and Frangiosa, D.K. (2021) *Going Gradeless, Grades 6–12: Shifting the Focus to Student Learning.* Corwin.

Butler, P. (2006) *A Review of the Literature on Portfolios and Electronic Portfolios.* https://creativecommons.org/licenses/by-nc-sa/2.5/

Carless, D. (2017) Scaling up assessment for learning: Progress and prospects. In D. Carless, S.M. Bridges, C.K.Y. Chan and R. Glofcheski (eds) *Scaling Up Assessment for Learning in Higher Education* (pp. 3–17). Springer.

Carless, D. and Boud, D. (2018) The development of student feedback literacy: Enabling uptake of feedback. *Assessment & Evaluation in Higher Education* 43 (8), 1315–1325.

Carless, D. and Winstone, N. (2020) Teacher feedback literacy and its interplay with student feedback literacy. *Teaching in Higher Education*. https://doi.org/10.1080/13562517.2020.1782372

Chang, C., Liang, C., Chou, P. and Liao, Y. (2018) Using e-Portfolio for learning goal setting to facilitate self-regulated learning of high school students. *Behaviour & Information Technology* 37 (12), 1237–1251.

Charles, S. (2022) Socio-constructivist pedagogy in physical and virtual spaces: The impacts and opportunities on dialogic learning in creative disciplines. *Architecture_MPS* 22 (1). https://doi.org/10.14324/111.444.amps.2022v22i1.001

Chaudhuri, T. and Cabau, B. (eds) (2018) *E-Portfolios in Higher Education: A Multidisciplinary Approach*. Springer.

Chen, P.P. and Bonner, S.M. (2020) A framework for classroom assessment, learning, and self-regulation. *Assessment in Education: Principles, Policy & Practice* 27 (4), 373–393.

Cheng, G. and Chau, J. (2009) Digital video for fostering self-reflection in an ePortfolio environment. *Learning, Media and Technology* 34 (4), 337–350.

Cheng, G. and Chau, J. (2013) Exploring the relationship between students' self-regulated learning ability and their ePortfolio achievement. *Internet and Higher Education* 17, 9–15.

Cheung, A. (2021) Language teaching during a pandemic: A case study of Zoom use by a secondary ESL teacher in Hong Kong. *RELC Journal*. https://doi.org/10.1177/0033688220981784

Cheung, A. (2022) Verbal and on-screen peer interactions of EFL learners during multimodal collaborative writing: A multiple case-study. *Journal of Second Language Writing* 58, 100931.

Cho, H. (2018) The pitfalls and promises of electronic portfolio assessment with secondary English language learners. In J. Perren, K.B. Kelch, J. Byun, S. Cervantes and S. Safari (eds) *Applications of CALL Theory in ESL and EFL Environments* (pp. 111–129). IGI Global.

Chong, I. (2017) Assessment dialogues between teachers and students in e-writing portfolios. *TESOL Journal* 8 (1), 240–243.

Cicchino, A., Efstathion, R. and Giarrusso, C. (2019) ePortfolio as curriculum: Revisualizing the composition process. In K.B. Yancey (ed.) *ePortfolio as Curriculum: Models and Practices for Developing Students' ePortfolio Literacy* (pp. 13–32). Stylus Publishing.

Clancy, M. and Gardner, J. (2017) Using digital portfolios to develop non-traditional domains in special education settings. *International Journal of ePortfolio* 7 (1), 93–100.

Clark, I. (2012) Formative assessment: Assessment is for self-regulated learning. *Educational Psychology Review* 24 (2), 205–249.

Clark, J.E. (2010) The digital imperative: Making the case for a 21st-century pedagogy. *Computers and Composition* 27, 27–35.

Clark, J.E. (2016) From selfies to self-representation in electronically mediated reflection: The evolving Gestalt effect in ePortfolios. In K.B. Yancey (ed.) *A Rhetoric of Reflection* (pp. 149–165). Utah State University Press.

Clarke, J.L. and Boud, D. (2018) Refocusing portfolio assessment: Curating for feedback and portrayal. *Innovations in Education and Teaching International* 55 (4), 479–486.

Cooper, A., DeLuca, C., Holden, M. and MacGregor, S. (2022) Emergency assessment: Rethinking classroom practices and priorities amid remote teaching. *Assessment in Education: Principles, Policy & Practice*. https://doi.org/10.1080/0969594X.2022.2069084

Crisol Moya, E., Gámiz Sánchez, V. and Romero Lopéz, M.A. (2021) University students' emotions when using e-Portfolios in virtual education environments. *Sustainability* 13, 6973. https://doi.org/10.3390/su13126973

Crusan, D. and Ruecker, T. (2022) *Linking Assignments to Assessments: A Guide for Teachers*. University of Michigan Press.

Cummins, P.W. and Davesne, C. (2009) Using electronic portfolios for second language assessment. *The Modern Language Journal* 93, 848–867.

Curriculum Development Council (2017) *English Language Education: Key Learning Area Curriculum Guide (Primary 1 – Secondary 6)*. Hong Kong.

Daniel, S.J. (2020) Education and the COVID-19 pandemic. *Prospects* 49, 91–96.

Dann, R. (2017) *Developing Feedback for Pupil Learning*. Routledge.

Daskalogiannaki, E. (2012) Developing and assessing EFL students' writing skills via a class-blog. *Research Papers in Language Teaching and Learning* 3 (1), 269–292.

Davison, C. and Leung, C. (2009) Current issues in English language teacher-based assessment. *TESOL Quarterly* 43 (3), 393–415.

De Bruin, H., van der Schaaf, M., Oosterbaan, A. and Prins, F. (2012) Secondary-school students' motivation for portfolio reflection. *Irish Educational Studies* 31 (4), 415–431.

De Nito, E., Gentile, T.A.R., Köhler, T., Misuraca, M. and Reina, R. (2022) E-learning experiences in tertiary education: Patterns and trends in research over the last 20 years. *Studies in Higher Education*. https://doi.org/10.1080/03075079.2022.2153246

Delett, J.S., Barnhardt, S. and Kevorkian, J.A. (2001) A framework for portfolio assessment in the foreign language classroom. *Foreign Language Annals* 34 (6), 559–565.

Deneen, C.C., Brown, G.T.L. and Carless, D. (2018) Students' conceptions of e-Portfolios as assessment and technology. *Innovations in Education and Teaching International* 55 (4), 487–496.

Dixson, D.D. and Worrell, F.C. (2016) Formative and summative assessment in the classroom. *Theory into Practice* 55 (2), 153–159.

Driessen, E.W., Muijtjens, A.M., Van Tartwijk, J. and Van der Vleuten, C.P. (2007) Web- or paper-based portfolios: Is there a difference? *Medical Education* 41 (11), 1067–1073.

Earl, L.M. (2013) *Assessment as Learning: Using Classroom Assessment to Maximize Student Learning* (2nd edn). Corwin.

Earl, L.M. and Katz, S. (2008) Getting to the core of learning: Using assessment for self-monitoring and self-regulation. In S. Swaffield (ed.) *Unlocking Assessment: Understanding for Reflection and Application* (pp. 90–104). Routledge.

Ene, E. and Upton, T.A. (2018) Synchronous and asynchronous teacher electronic feedback and learner uptake in ESL composition. *Journal of Second Language Writing* 41, 1–13.

Eynon, B. and Gambino, L.M. (2017) *High-Impact ePortfolio Practice: A Catalyst for Student, Faculty, and Institutional Learning*. Stylus Publishing.

Eynon, R. (2021) Utilising a critical realist lens to conceptualise digital inequality: The experiences of less well-off internet users. *Social Science Computer Review*. https://doi.org/10.1177/08944393211069662

Fabian, K. and Topping, K.J. (2019) Putting "mobile" into mathematics: Results of a randomised controlled trial. *Contemporary Educational Psychology* 59, 101783.

Fahey, K., Lawrence, J. and Paratore, J. (2007) Using electronic portfolios to make learning public. *Journal of Adolescent & Adult Literacy* 50 (6), 460–471.

Farahian, M., Avarzamani, F. and Rajabi, Y. (2021) Reflective thinking in an EFL writing course: To what level do portfolios improve reflection in writing? *Thinking Skills and Creativity* 39, 100759.

Farrell, O. (2020) From portafoglio to e-Portfolio: The evolution of portfolio in higher education. *Journal of Interactive Media in Education* 19 (1), 1–14. https://doi.org/10.5334/jime.574

Farrell, T.S.C. and Stanclik, C. (2021) "COVID-19 is an opportunity to rediscover our-selves": Reflections of a novice EFL teacher in Central America. *RELC Journal.* https://doi.org/10.1177/0033688220981778

Fathi, J. and Rahimi, M. (2022) Electronic writing portfolio in a collaborative writing environment: Its impact on EFL students' writing performance. *Computer Assisted Language Learning.* https://doi.org/10.1080/09588221.2022.2097697

Fukuda, S.T., Lander, B.W. and Pope, C.J. (2022) Formative assessment for learning how to learn: Exploring university student learning experiences. *RELC Journal* 53 (1), 118–133.

Gacs, A., Goertler, S. and Spasova, S. (2020) Planned online language education versus crisis-prompted online language teaching: Lessons for the future. *Foreign Language Annals* 53 (2), 380–392.

Gan, L. and Lam, R. (2022) A review on language assessment literacy: Trends, foci and contributions. *Language Assessment Quarterly* 19 (5), 503–525.

Goh, C.C.M. and Burns, A. (2012) *Teaching Speaking: A Holistic Approach.* Cambridge University Press.

Goh, C.C.M. and Vandergrift, L. (2021) *Teaching and Learning Second Language Listening: Metacognition in Action* (2nd edn). Routledge.

Green, A. (2020) *Exploring Language Assessment and Testing: Language in Action* (2nd edn). Routledge.

Green, A. (2022) *L2 Writing Assessment: An Evolutionary Perspective.* Palgrave MacMillan.

Gu, P.Y. (2021) *Classroom-based Formative Assessment.* Foreign Language Teaching and Research Press.

Gu, P.Y. and Lam, R. (2023) Developing assessment literacy for classroom-based forma-tive assessment. *Chinese Journal of Applied Linguistics* 46 (2), 155–161.

Guo, W.Y. and Yan, Z. (2019) Formative and summative assessment in Hong Kong pri-mary schools: Students' attitudes matter. *Assessment in Education: Principles, Policy & Practice* 26 (6), 675–699.

Guskey, T.R. (2022) Can grades be an effective form of feedback? *Phi Delta Kappan* 104 (3), 36–41.

Guskey, T.R. and Brookhart, S.M. (2019) *What We Know About Grading: What Works, What Doesn't, and What's Next?* ASCD.

Hadwin, A., Jarvela, S. and Miller, M. (2018) Self-regulation, co-regulation, and shared regulation in collaborative learning environment. In D.H. Schunk and J.A. Greene (eds) *Handbook of Self-Regulation of Learning and Performance* (2nd edn, pp. 83–106). Routledge.

Hamp-Lyons, L. and Condon, W. (2000) *Assessing the Portfolio: Issues for Research, Theory and Practice.* Hampton Press.

Händel, M., Wimmer, B. and Ziegler, A. (2020) E-Portfolio use and its effects on exam performance – A field study. *Studies in Higher Education* 45 (2), 258–270.

Hanh, L.T.T. and Huong, T.T.B. (2021) Applying Flipgrid-based portfolio to improve Vietnamese EFL high school students' speaking scores. *3L The Southeast Asian Journal of English Language Studies* 27 (4), 85–100. https://doi.org/10.17576/3L-2021 -2704-07

Harlen, W. (2005) Teachers' summative practices and assessment for learning – Tensions and synergies. *The Curriculum Journal* 16 (2), 207–223.

Harmer, J. (2015) *The Practice of English Language Teaching* (5th edn). Pearson.

Hattie, J. and Timperley, H. (2007) The power of feedback. *Review of Educational Research* 77, 81–112.

Hinkel, E. (2006) Current perspectives on teaching the four skills. *TESOL Quarterly* 40 (1), 109–131.

Hockly, N. and Dudeney, G. (2018) Current and future digital trends in ELT. *RELC Journal* 49 (2), 164–178.

Hung, S.T.A. (2012) A washback study on e-Portfolio assessment in an English as a foreign language teacher preparation program. *Computer Assisted Language Learning* 25 (1), 21–36.

Hung, S.T.A. and Huang, H.T.D. (2010) E-Portfolio-based language learning and assessment. *The International Journal of Learning* 17 (7), 313–335.

Hyland, K. (2021) *Teaching and Researching Writing* (4th edn). Routledge.

Jones, N. and Saville, N. (2016) *Learning Oriented Assessment: A Systemic Approach.* Cambridge University Press.

Kang, Q., Lu, J. and Xu, J. (2021) Is e-reading environmentally more sustainable than conventional reading? Evidence from a systematic literature review. *Library & Information Science Research* 43 (3), 101105.

Karlin, M., Ozogul, G., Miles, S. and Heide, S. (2016) The practical application of e-Portfolios in K-12 classrooms: An exploration of three web 2.0 tools by three teachers. *TechTrends* 60, 374–380.

Kelly, N. (2018) Student perceptions and attitudes towards the use of Facebook to support the acquisition of Japanese as a second language. *Language Learning in Higher Education* 8 (2), 217–237.

Klenowski, V. (2009) Assessment for learning revisited: An Asia-Pacific perspective. *Assessment in Education: Principles, Policy & Practice* 16 (3), 263–268.

Koretz, D. (1998) Large-scale portfolio assessment in the US: Evidence pertaining to the quality of measurement. *Assessment in Education: Principles, Policy & Practice* 5 (3), 309–334.

Kuepper-Tetzel, C.E. and Gardner, P.L. (2021) Effects of temporary mark withholding on academic performance. *Psychology Learning & Teaching* 20 (3), 405–419.

Kusuma, I.P.I. and Waluyo, B. (2023) Enacting e-Portfolios in online English-speaking courses: Speaking performance and self-efficacy. *Iranian Journal of Language Teaching Research* 11 (1), 75–95.

Lam, R. (2013) Formative use of summative tests: Using test preparation to promote performance and self-regulation. *The Asia-Pacific Education Researcher* 22 (1), 69–78.

Lam, R. (2015a) Feedback about self-regulation: Does it remain an 'unfinished business' in portfolio assessment of writing? *TESOL Quarterly* 49 (2), 402–413.

Lam, R. (2015b) Understanding EFL students' development of self-regulated learning in a process-oriented writing course. *TESOL Journal* 6 (3), 527–553.

Lam, R. (2017a) Enacting feedback utilization from a task-specific perspective. *The Curriculum Journal* 28 (2), 266–282.

Lam, R. (2017b) Taking stock of portfolio assessment scholarship: From research to practice. *Assessing Writing* 31, 84–97.

Lam, R. (2018a) *Portfolio Assessment for the Teaching and Learning of Writing.* Springer.

Lam, R. (2018b) Promoting self-reflection in writing: A showcase portfolio approach. In A. Burns and J. Siegel (eds) *International Perspectives on Teaching Skills in ELT* (pp. 219–231). Palgrave MacMillan.

Lam, R. (2018c) Understanding assessment as learning in writing classrooms: The case of portfolio assessment. *Iranian Journal of Language Teaching Research* 6 (3), 19–36.

Lam, R. (2019) *Using Portfolios in Language Teaching.* SEAMEO Regional Language Centre.

Lam, R. (2020) Why reinvent the wheel? E-Portfolios are for learning. *ELT Journal* 74 (4), 488–491.

Lam, R. (2021a) From paper to digital portfolios: Evolution of writing portfolio-based research – 1980–2020 [Paper presentation]. 55th RELC International Conference on Sustainable Language Education: Standards, Strategies and Systems, Southeast Asian Ministers of Education Organization - Regional Language Centre, Singapore.

Lam, R. (2021b) Using ePortfolios to promote assessment of, for, as learning in EFL writing. *The European Journal of Applied Linguistics and TEFL* 10 (1), 101–120.

Lam, R. (2022a) E-Portfolios for self-regulated and co-regulated learning: A review. *Frontiers in Psychology* 13, 1079385. https://doi.org/10.3389/fpsyg.2022.1079385

Lam, R. (2022b) Test usefulness of e-Portfolios: An alternative approach during and beyond the pandemic. In K. Sadeghi (ed.) *Technology-Assisted Language Assessment in Diverse Contexts: Lessons from the Transition to Online Testing During COVID-19* (pp. 181–195). Routledge.

Lam, R. (2022c) Understanding the usefulness of e-Portfolios: Linking artefacts, reflection, and validation. *International Review of Applied Linguistics in Language Teaching.* https://doi.org/10.1515/iral-2022-0052

Lam, R. (2023) E-Portfolios: What we know, what we don't, and what we need to know. *RELC Journal* 54 (1), 208–215. https://doi.org/10.1177/0033688220974102

Lam, R. and Lee, I. (2010) Balancing the dual functions of portfolio assessment. *ELT Journal* 64 (1), 54–64.

Lam, R., Lau, M. and Wong, J. (2023) E-Portfolios as a technology-enabled assessment: Surviving or accommodating COVID-19. In K. Sadeghi, M. Thomas and F. Ghaderi (eds) *Technology-Enhanced Language Teaching and Learning: Lessons from the COVID-19 Pandemic* (pp. 183–196). Bloomsbury.

Lau, A.M.S. (2016) 'Formative good, summative bad?' – A review of the dichotomy in assessment literature. *Journal of Further and Higher Education* 40 (4), 509–525.

Le, A.N.N., Bo, L.K. and Nguyen, N.M.T. (2023) Canva-based e-Portfolios in L2 writing instructions: Investigating the effects and students' attitudes. *Computer Assisted Language Learning* 42 (1), 41–62.

Lee, A.V.Y. (2023) Supporting students' generation of feedback in large-scale online course with artificial intelligence-enabled evaluation. *Studies in Educational Evaluation* 77, 101250.

Lee, I. (2021a) Teaching writing in Hong Kong: Where are we? *Composition Studies* 49 (3), 155–159.

Lee, I. (2021b) The development of feedback literacy for writing teachers. *TESOL Quarterly* 55 (3), 1048–1059.

Lee, I., Mak, P. and Yuan, R. (2019) Assessment as learning in primary writing classrooms: An exploratory study. *Studies in Educational Evaluation* 62, 72–81.

Lee, Y.J. (2022) Language learning affordances of Instagram and TikTok. *Innovation in Language Learning and Teaching.* https://doi.org/10.1080/17501229.2022.2051517

Li, J. and Li, M. (2022) Assessing L2 writing in the digital age: Opportunities and challenges. *Journal of Second Language Writing* 57 (8), 100913. https://doi.org/10.1016/j.jslw.2022.100913

Li, J., Mak, L., Hunter, B. and Cunningham, T. (2022) Structured instructional design for integrated language skill development: College students' perspectives on collaborative reading-to-write activities using a cloud-based tool. *Language Teaching Research.* https://doi.org/10.1177/13621688221142297

Li, L. (2017) *New Technologies and Language Learning.* Palgrave.

Li, M. (2021) *Researching and Teaching Second Language Writing in the Digital Age.* Palgrave Macmillan.

Li, M. and Zhang, M. (2023) Collaborative writing in L2 classrooms. A research agenda. *Language Teaching* 56 (1), 94–112.

Ligado, F.N.G., Palattao, J.T., Gamis, J.L., Felix, C.C. and Bautista, R.G. (2022) Teachers' affordances in using academic e-Portfolio. *American Journal of Educational Research* 10 (5), 355–360.

Light, T.P., Chen, H.L. and Ittelson, J.C. (2012) *Documenting Learning with ePortfolios: A Guide for College Instructors.* Jossey-Bass.

Luić, L. (2020) Challenges of digital age curriculum convergence [Paper presentation]. *ICERI 2020 Proceedings.* http://doi.org/10.21125/iceri.2020.1383

Madden, K., Collins, E. and Lander, P. (2019) Nursing students' perspectives on ePortfolios: Themes and preferences compared with paper-based experiences. *International Journal of ePortfolio* 9 (2), 87–96.

Magno, C. and Lizada, G.S. (2015) Features of classroom formative assessment. *Educational Measurement and Evaluation Review* 6, 23–31.

Mak, P. and Wong, K.M. (2018) Self-regulation through portfolio assessment in writing classrooms. *ELT Journal* 72 (1), 49–61.

Mazloomi, S. and Khabiri, M. (2018) The impact of self-assessment on language learners' writing skill. *Innovations in Education and Teaching International* 55 (1), 91–100.

McDonald, B. (2012) Portfolio assessment: Direct from the classroom. *Assessment & Evaluation in Higher Education* 37 (3), 335–347.

McLaren, S.V. (2012) Assessment is for learning: Supporting feedback. *International Journal of Technology and Design Education* 22 (2), 227–245.

McLeod, J.K. and Vasinda, S. (2009) Electronic portfolios: Perspectives of students, teachers and parents. *Education and Information Technologies* 14 (1), 29–38.

Meyer, E.J., Abrami, P.C., Wade, A. and Scherzer, R. (2011) Electronic portfolios in the classroom. Factors impacting teachers' integration of new technologies and new pedagogies. *Technology, Pedagogy and Education* 20 (2), 191–207.

Moorhouse, B.L. and Beaumont, A.M. (2020) Involving parents in their children's school-based English language writing using digital learning. *RELC Journal* 51 (2), 259–267.

Moya, S.S. and O'Malley, J.M. (2001) A portfolio assessment model for ESL. *The Journal of Educational Issues of Language Minority Students* 13, 13–36.

Nation, I.S.P. (2009) *Teaching ESL/EFL Reading and Writing*. Routledge.

Navarre, A. (2019) *Technology-Enhanced Teaching and Learning of Chinese as a Foreign Language*. Routledge.

Nevisi, R.B. and Hosseinpur, R.M. (2022) Task-based speaking assessment in an EFL academic context: A case of summative and formative assessment. *Research in English Language Pedagogy* 10 (2), 256–276.

Nguyen, T.T., Richardson, T., Nguyen, A.N., Vu, T.N. and Dang, T.T.H. (2023) A systematic review of potential opportunities and challenges to the use of portfolios in Vietnam as an assessment tool. *Innovation in Language Learning and Teaching* 17 (5), 894–908.

Nicol, D., Serbati, A. and Tracchi, M. (2019) Competence development and portfolios: Promoting reflection through peer review. *AISHE-J* 11 (2), 1–13.

Nicolaidou, I. (2010) Using a weblog as an ePortfolio tool in elementary school essay writing. In P. Escudeiro (ed.) *The 9th European Conference on e-Learning* (pp. 417–426). Instituto Superior de Engenhanria de Porto.

Nicolaidou, I. (2013) E-Portfolios supporting primary students' writing performance and peer feedback. *Computers & Education* 68, 404–415.

Nunan, D. (2012) *Learner-Centred English Language Education: The Selected Works of David Nunan*. Routledge.

O'Byrne, B. and Murrell, S. (2014) Evaluating multimodal literacies in student blogs. *British Journal of Educational Technology* 45 (5), 926–940.

Osorio-Saez, E.M., Eryilmaz, N. and Sandoval-Hernandez, A. (2021) Parents' acceptance of educational technology: Lessons from around the world. *Frontiers in Psychology* 12, 719430. https://doi.org/10.3389/fpsyg.2021.719430

Pintrich, P.R. and Zusho, A. (2002) Student motivation and self-regulated learning in the college classroom. In J.C. Smart and W.G. Tierney (eds) *Higher Education: Handbook of Theory and Research* (vol. 17). Agathon Press.

Pourdana, N. and Tavassoli, K. (2022) Differential impacts of e-Portfolio assessment on language learners' engagement modes and genre-based writing improvement. *Language Testing in Asia* 12 (7). https://doi.org/10.1186/s40468-022-00156-7

Purnama, A.D. (2017) Incorporating memes and Instagram to enhance students' participation. *Language and Language Teaching Journal* 20 (1), 1–14.

Rafalow, M.H. and Puckett, C. (2022) Sorting machines: Digital technology and categorical inequality in education. *Educational Researcher* 51 (4), 274–278.

Renwick, M. (2017) *Digital Portfolios in the Classroom: Showcasing and Assessing Student Work*. Association for Supervision and Curriculum Development.

Richards, J.C. (2013) Curriculum approaches in language teaching: Forward, central, and backward design. *RELC Journal* 44 (1), 5–33.

Ritzhaupt, A.D., Singh, O., Seyferth, T. and Dedrick, R.F. (2008) Development of the electronic portfolio student perspective instrument: An e-Portfolio integration initiative. *Journal of Computing in Higher Education* 19 (2), 47–71.

Roy, D. and Putatunda, T. (2020) Deconstructing language classrooms: A study of digital learning in the Indian context. *The IUP Journal of English Studies* 15 (3), 15–25.

Russell, V. and Murphy-Judy, K. (2021) *Teaching Language Online: A Guide for Designing, Developing, and Delivering Online, Blended, and Flipped Language Courses*. Routledge.

Sadeghi, K. (2021) *Assessing Second Language Reading: Insights from Cloze Tests*. Springer.

Saeed, M.A. and Al Qunayeer, H.S. (2022) Exploring teacher interactive e-feedback on students' writing through Google Docs: Factors promoting interactivity and potential for learning. *The Language Learning Journal* 50 (3), 360–377.

Sailer, M., Murböck, J. and Fischer, F. (2021) Digital learning in schools: What does it take beyond digital technology? *Teaching and Teacher Education* 103, 103346.

Sasai, L. (2017) Self-regulated learning and the use of online portfolios: A social cognitive perspective. *Journal of Educational and Social Research* 7 (2), 55–65.

Scott, T. (2005) Creating the subject of portfolios: Reflective writing and the conveyance of institutional prerogatives. *Written Communication* 22 (3), 3–35.

Segaran, M.K. and Hasim, Z. (2021) Self-regulated learning through ePortfolio: A meta-analysis. *Malaysian Journal of Learning and Instruction* 18 (1), 131–156.

Sharifi, M., Soleimani, H. and Jafarigohar, M. (2017) E-Portfolio evaluation and vocabulary learning: Moving from pedagogy to andragogy. *British Journal of Educational Technology* 48 (6), 1441–1450.

Shepherd, C.E. and Skrabut, S. (2011) Rethinking electronic portfolios to promote sustainability among teachers. *TechTrends* 55 (5), 31–38.

Silver, N. (2016) Reflection in digital spaces: Publication, conversation, collaboration. In K.B. Yancey (ed.) *A Rhetoric of Reflection* (pp. 166–200). Utah State University Press.

Siu, F. (2013) The incorporation of ePortfolios into five EFL courses – Barriers encountered in the diffusion of technology. *Journal of Interactive Learning Research* 24 (2), 211–231.

Skar, G.B., Graham, S. and Rijlaarsdam, G. (2022) Formative writing assessment for change – Introduction to the special issue. *Assessment in Education: Principles, Policy & Practice* 29 (2), 121–126.

Song, B.K. (2021) E-Portfolio implementation: Examining learners' perception of usefulness, self-directed learning process and value of learning. *Australasian Journal of Educational Technology* 37 (1), 68–81.

Springfield, E. (2001) Comparing electronic and paper portfolios. In B.L. Cambridge, S. Kahn, D.P. Tompkins and K.B. Yancey (eds) *Electronic Portfolios: Emerging Practices in Student, Faculty, and Institutional Learning* (pp. 76–87). Stylus Publishing.

Stefani, L., Mason, R. and Pegler, C. (2007) *The Educational Potential of e-Portfolios: Supporting Personal Development and Reflective Learning*. Routledge.

Sun, Y.C. and Yang, F.Y. (2015) I help, therefore, I learn: Service learning on Web 2.0 in EFL speaking class. *Computer Assisted Language Learning* 28 (3), 202–219.

Swaffield, S. (2011) Getting to the heart of authentic assessment for learning. *Assessment in Education: Principles, Policy & Practice* 18 (4), 433–449.

Teng, L.S. (2022) Explicit strategy-based instruction in L2 writing contexts: A perspective of self-regulated learning and formative assessment. *Assessing Writing* 53, 100645.

Teng, L.S. and Zhang, L.J. (2022) Can self-regulation be transferred to second/foreign language learning and teaching? Current status, controversies, and future directions. *Applied Linguistics* 43 (3), 587–595.

Thornbury, S. (2012) Speaking instruction. In A. Burns and J.C. Richards (eds) *The Cambridge Guide to Pedagogy and Practice in Second Language Teaching* (pp. 198–206). Cambridge University Press.

Tondeur, J., Van Braak, J., Ertmer, P.A. and Ottenbreit-Leftwich, A. (2017) Understanding the relationship between teachers' pedagogical beliefs and technology use in education: A systematic review of qualitative evidence. *Educational Technology Research and Development* 65 (3), 555–575.

Tsagari, D. (2021) Language assessment literacy: Concepts, challenges, and prospects. In S. Hidri (ed.) *Perspectives on Language Assessment Literacy: Challenges for Improved Student Learning* (pp. 13–32). Routledge.

Vahedi, Z., Zannella, L. and Want, S.C. (2021) Students' use of information and communication technologies in the classroom: Uses, restriction, and integration. *Active Learning in Higher Education* 22 (3), 215–228.

Vygotsky, L. (1978) *Mind in Society: The Development of Higher Psychological Processes.* Harvard University Press.

Walland, E. and Shaw, S. (2022) E-Portfolios in teaching, learning and assessment: Tensions in theory and praxis. *Technology, Pedagogy and Education* 31 (3), 363–379.

Wang, L. and Lee, I. (2021) L2 learners' agentic engagement in an assessment as learning-focused writing classroom. *Assessing Writing* 50, 100571.

Wang, Y. (2021) In-service teachers' perceptions of technology integration and practices in a Japanese university context. *The JALT CALL Journal* 17 (1), 45–71.

Wiliam, D. (2011) What is assessment for learning? *Studies in Educational Evaluation* 37, 3–14.

Wilson, C., Slade, C., Kirby, M., Downer, T., Fisher, M. and Nuessler, S. (2018) Digital ethics and the use of ePortfolio: A scoping review of the literature. *International Journal of ePortfolio* 8 (2), 115–125.

Winstone, N. and Carless, D. (2019) *Designing Effective Feedback Processes in Higher Education: A Learning-Focused Approach.* Routledge.

Woodward, H. and Nanlohy, P. (2004) Digital portfolios: Fact or fashion? *Assessment & Evaluation in Higher Education* 29 (2), 227–238.

Wuetherick, B. and Dickinson, J. (2015) Why ePortfolios? Student perceptions of ePortfolio use in continuing education learning environments. *International Journal of ePortfolio* 5 (1), 39–53.

Yancey, K.B. (1996) The electronic portfolio: Shifting paradigms. *Computers and Composition* 13, 259–262.

Yancey, K.B. (2001) Digitalized student portfolios. In B.L. Cambridge, S. Kahn, D.P. Tompkins and K.B. Yancey (eds) *Electronic Portfolios: Emerging Practices in Student, Faculty, and Institutional Learning* (pp. 15–30). Stylus Publishing.

Yancey, K.B. (2004) Postmodernism, palimpsest, and portfolios: Theoretical issues in the representation of student work. *College Composition and Communication* 55 (4), 738–761.

Yancey, K.B. (2009) Electronic portfolios a decade into the twenty-first century: What we know, what we need to know. *Peer Review* 11 (1), 28–32.

Yancey, K.B. (2015) Grading ePortfolios: Tracing two approaches, their advantages, and their disadvantages. *Theory into Practice* 54, 301–308.

Yancey, K.B. (ed.) (2019) *ePortfolio as Curriculum: Models and Practices for Developing Students' ePortfolio Literacy.* Stylus Publishing.

Yancey, K.B. and Weiser, I. (eds) (1997) *Situating Portfolios: Four Perspectives.* Utah State University Press.

Yancey, K.B., McElroy, S.J. and Powers, E. (2013) Composing, networks, and electronic portfolios: Notes toward a theory of assessing ePortfolios. In H.A. McKee and D.N. DeVoss (eds) *Digital Writing Assessment and Evaluation* (pp. 1–32). Utah State University Press.

Yin, S.K. (2022) A study of the effects of thematic language teaching on the promotion of multimedia design students' listening and speaking skills. *Frontiers in Psychology* 13, 915145. https://doi.org/10.3389/fpsyg.2022.915145

Zheng, Y. and Barrot, J.S. (2022) Social media as an e-Portfolio platform: Effects on L2 learners' speaking performance. *Language Learning & Technology* 26 (1), 1–19.

Zhu, Q. and To, J. (2022) Proactive receiver roles in peer feedback dialogue: Facilitating receivers' self-regulation and co-regulating providers' learning. *Assessment & Evaluation in Higher Education* 47 (8), 1200–1212.

Zimmerman, B.J. (2002) Becoming a self-regulated learner: An overview. *Theory into Practice* 42 (2), 64–70.

Index

Note: References in *italics* are to figures, those in **bold** to tables; 'n' refers to chapter notes.

For Product Safety Concerns and Information please contact our EU Authorised Representative:

Easy Access System Europe

Mustamäe tee 50

10621 Tallinn

Estonia

gpsr.requests@easproject.com

www.ingramcontent.com/pod-product-compliance
Lightning Source LLC
Chambersburg PA
CBHW071137050326
40690CB00008B/1491